REVIEWS OF THE FIRST EDITION

'Magnificently detailed, a rich and absorbing read,' - BookNews

'Wonderfully entertaining and not without some fascinating original scholarship,' - Libris Press

OTHER BOOKS by Julian Dutton

Keeping Quiet: Visual Comedy in the Age of Sound

'A custard pie in the face of those who say slapstick is dead, by the go-to writer of British visual comedy,' - Harry Hill.

Water Gypsies: a History of Life on Britain's Rivers & Canals

'A beautiful book. Julian Dutton grew up on the water, and he's the perfect guide to the life aquatic. There could be no better or more informative guide to a history of life aboard,' - Samuel West.

The Parade's Gone By: everyday life in Britain in the twentieth century.

'A history of Britain like you've never read before,' - History Now.

SHAKESPEARE'S JOURNEY HOME

FURNIVAL BOOKS

A TRAVELLER'S GUIDE
THROUGH ELIZABETHAN ENGLAND

First published 2015 by Matador

This edition published by Furnival Books 2024.

© Julian Dutton

The right of Julian Dutton to be be identified as the Author of this work has been asserted in accordance with the Copyright, Designs and Patents Act 1988.

All rights reserved. No part of this book may be reprinted or reproduced or utilised in any form or by any electronic, mechanical or other means, now known or hereafter invented, including photocopying or recording, or in any information storage or retrieval system, without permission in writing from the publishers.

British Library Cataloguing in Publication Data.

A catalogue record for this book is available from the British Library.

ISBN 978-1-3999-8398-3

FURNIVAL BOOKS

CONTENTS

Introduction

1 Shakespeare's Neighbourhood: Shoreditch & Bishopsgate
1

2 Sick with the working of my thoughts:
Setting off.
19

3 My Grief lies Onward: Bishopsgate to Carter Lane.
33

4 Shakespeare's Horse.
55

5 To the Edge: Newgate to Tyburn.
61

6 The Killing Fields: Tyburn to Shepherd's Bush.
91

7 The Elizabethan Landscape.
97

8 Market Gardens & Inns: Acton & Ealing.
101

9 The Wilds of Southall & Hayes, & bustling Uxbridge.
113

10 Traveller's Rest: Uxbridge to Beaconsfield.
127

11 Bandit Country: High Wycombe to Stokenchurch.
143

12 Stokenchurch to Wheatley.
169

13 Friends & Godsons: Oxford.
187

14 Sheep & Fairs: Oxford to Chipping Norton.
197

15 Ancient England: the Poet & Nature.
213

16 Warwickshire Made Me.
223

17 Hearth & Home: Stratford.
239

Epilogue
249

ILLUSTRATIONS

All illustrations are of scenes and buildings Shakespeare would have seen en route from London to Stratford. All photographs and illustrations have been sourced from the public domain and are fully credited. If there have been any omissions please notify the publisher and these will be rectified in future editions.

DEDICATION

For my Father for instilling in me his love of landscape & history, for the Wilmott family, & to Jack, Florence & Siw for their unfailing love & encouragement.

INTRODUCTION

It has become customary when introducing yet another book on Shakespeare to present the reader with an apology. Russell Fraser in his book *Young Shakespeare* says the playwright's "...biography is hardly barren of facts, and a multitude crowd its margins." This book, such as it is, attempts to occupy those margins. For it is in the suburbs, the hinterlands of the subject, that possibilities for new discoveries, illuminations and fresh approaches lie.

Even after all the plays and biographies of Shakespeare have been read, a mysterious hunger lingers. Why? It is perhaps a symptom of the traditional "enigma of Shakespeare," the notion that he never fully revealed himself in his works but submitted so wholeheartedly to the truth of his characters that - unlike, say, Ben Jonson - his own personality absented itself from the plays, leaving us with greater drama but also with vague, troubling feelings: at best a sense of awe, at worst, a sense of puzzlement.

It has long been a dream of mine to discover, in an old attic room, reels of film containing the grainy, flickering images of a time traveller's journey back to Elizabethan England - footage of the first ever performance of Burbage's Hamlet, the crowning of James I, the burning of the Globe Theatre in 1612...

I can confidently assert that I will never find such a film, and if I ever claim to have done so please feel free to immure me in the nearest asylum for unhinged literary historians.

In one sense, of course, we already possess such film – the work itself. Shakespeare's tailor in "King John" rushing out of his workshop with his slippers on the wrong feet in his haste to speak to his friend the smith is without doubt an image recorded from life, no less vivid than if it had been captured on celluloid. Indeed, had he been born in the twentieth century Shakespeare would probably not have been living in Holland Park like Pinter but in Hollywood like Raymond Chandler or Orson Welles. His was a cinematic intelligence; it might be said that Shakespeare invented cross-cutting from scene to scene, the basic staple of film grammar. In the latter half of the sixteenth century, however, his eye was his camera, his quill his celluloid.

So we have the work, in Jonson's words "not for his age, but for all time," yet despite the corpus itself mirroring its age in a cinematic manner, a mysterious hunger still lingers ... *one is left wanting more of the man himself...*

The number of books written about Shakespeare must now run into hundreds of thousands and their production shows no sign of abating: James Shapiro's account of one year in the playwright's life, "1599," Stephen Greenblatt's "Will in the World," Park Honan's comprehensive "Life," Peter Ackroyd's and Bill Bryson's biographies, and now Charles's Nicholl's intense local detail in "The Lodger: Shakespeare in Silver Street" - all are buckling the nation's bookshelves as I write. The documentary evidence of his life is valuable and fascinating, yet disappointingly finite. So a challenge presents itself: how can we get closer to Shakespeare the man without examining for the thousandth time the scant documents in which his name appears? How can we, in short, develop a *new* and fruitful method of biography?

With the documentary evidence of Shakespeare's life so paltry, though ampler than other playwrights of his age, biographers are constrained to pore over the same crumbling fragments like magpies squabbling over carrion.

Yet there is a limit to what a hundred writers can say about one document in the public record office; moreover, all such comments must of necessity be interpretation. Conjecture has its place – the beauty lies in the quality of the response.

One possibly fruitful way might be not to simply re-examine for the thousandth time the few documents in existence that contain his name. Another way to crawl inside his skin might be to explore one of the most dominating and incontrovertible facts we know about him - that one or more times a year he travelled home, from London to Stratford.

Much in Shakespearean biography is guesswork: his journey from London to Stratford is not. As Russell Fraser says, Jonson's eulogy in his preface to the First Folio that Shakespeare was "for all time," has perhaps blinkered future appraisals by studying him purely as some kind of transcendent figure rather than flesh and blood. We have to approach Shakespeare's life as we might approach our own – physical, sensual, material, historical. Any other approach and we are simply imparting to him obsessions and meanings that are refractions of ourselves. Shakespeare was a man whose urges and obligations were the same as any man who has ever lived.

I wanted to write a book on Shakespeare that no one else had written. I wanted to add something original to Shakespeariana - not an easy task. So the aim of this book is very simple - to recreate Shakespeare's travels from his lodgings in the City of London to Stratford-upon-Avon in Warwickshire, and as much as possible apply such an historical precision to the journey as may afford a sense of what it must have been like to be Shakespeare travelling through his England.

Many biographers have touched on this journey casually in their books, but there has never been a whole volume devoted to the journey. John W. Hales wrote an article in 1884, "From Stratford to London," in his "Notes and Essays on Shakespeare," a wonderful high-Victorian eulogy to the countryside and historical lore of the England Shakespeare would have passed through on his way to London, but his article is only fifteen pages long and his journey peters out at Uxbridge.

Dominic Dromgoole, the Artistic Director of the Globe Theatre, allotted the latter part of his book "Will & Me: How Shakespeare took over my life," to a recreation of the playwright's "walk" south. However, wonderful though this section of his book is, he makes no claims at all to be historically accurate, as his route follows footpaths and fields rather than the established highways, and even drops down to the Thames after Oxford. His journey mirrors, indeed, the recent "official" footpath called "Shakespeare's Way," the officiators of which are blatantly honest about their route being purely imaginary, focussing as it does on the picturesque and touristic rather than the historical and practical. And Russell A. Fraser's reconstruction of the playwright's walk from Stratford, in his book "Young Shakespeare," is equally imaginative.

In the present book I have concentrated ruthlessly on the historical, and even though this may sacrifice at times a little of the picturesque – passing as I do through Uxbridge, for example, rather than ambling pleasantly along the fragrant towpath at Marlow – I for one feel a far greater frisson from being able to sit in the front parlour of an inn that Shakespeare sat in, or feel the stonework of a bridge we know he crossed, or pass through woods I know he passed through, than simply have a pleasing journey. From the very first I decided to trace his exact route from his lodgings in Bishopsgate, through the streets of London, along the great western highway out into the suburbs of Acton, Northcote, Southall and Uxbridge, meeting up with the A40 to Beaconsfield, High Wycombe and Oxford, and thence north through the villages and hills of the Midlands, all the way to the town where he was born - en route seeing the fields and farms he saw, the remains of the buildings he passed, and maybe even meeting the descendants of people he knew.

I examine every building he would have seen, study every meadow and farm he passed, trace each inn he would have stayed in - and some do still stand - and discover precisely who would have been living in each village and town he travelled through on that day.

My aim was chiefly to get close to the life of the man by spending several days "being him," doing something we know he definitely did. But as the journey progressed another goal materialised: to discover how much remains of that Elizabethan England he knew, what buildings are still standing, what fields and farms, what villages and towns. Were there any clues along the route, any nuance of landscape, any landmark, any local historical character, which may have found their way into the texts of the greatest literature ever written? The great local historian W.G. Hoskins declared that one of the principal omissions committed by those engaged in historical research is, simply, the evidence of their own eyes. In being wedded to documents and books, we tend to ignore the fact that history is still living all around us.

The journey threw up some remarkable surprises and many discoveries. Although far more remains of Elizabethan England than one might think, much detective work is required to find it.

And much imaginative recreation, built of course on historical study. The journey is a work of time travel, an archaeology of the eye. To recreate the England of Elizabeth you have first to destroy, strip away, dismantle, operate a huge demolition ball of the mind – smash the shopping malls and the service stations and the skyscrapers, peel away the tarmac, root up the traffic signage, obliterate the shop-fronts.

Then slowly build anew... sow grass in the streets, plant thyme on banks, erect gleaming whitewashed wattle and daub shops and buildings, clean white palaces with names like Nonesuch and York House; rut the roads, freshen up the streams, sweeten the air...

CHAPTER ONE

SHAKESPEARE'S NEIGHBOURHOOD
- SHOREDITCH & BISHOPSGATE

Any journey in search of Shakespeare's early life in London begins in the oddly featureless suburb of Shoreditch on the northern fringes of the City. For it was here that four hundred and twenty years ago in the late 1580's a young man in his early twenties moved from his father's gloving shop in Warwickshire to try his luck as a novice actor and playwright for the emerging public theatre industry. After ten years hard graft, he had become the greatest writer ever to have lived.

For most of his working life in the capital we know precisely where Shakespeare lived, principally because of the tax records relating to the parishes in which he dwelt, including a court summons for tax evasion in the ward of St. Helen's, Bishopsgate.

When he arrived here in the late 1580's - staying probably in an actor's lodging-house in Holywell Lane - the neighbourhood of Shoreditch was down-at-heel, rough, poor. Today, it's difficult not to reach the conclusion that it still is, though nearby Hoxton with its reputation as the home of shabby-chic Brit-art is rippling eastwards with its smart cafes and boutiques. Alleyways of cracked flagstones, a ramshackle stationery shop, an Afro-Caribbean café, a massage parlour, hoodies passing by on the pavement like cowed yet malevolent goblins, tramps cooking gently in the Sunday sunshine on the bench opposite St. Leonard's church in Shoreditch High Street...

In 1587 it probably wasn't much different; a country highway for northbound traffic threading its way from the City Wall at Bishopsgate, bordered by lodging houses, tenements, crudely built shops: a straggling suburban sprawl minutes away from meadow, field and stream but becoming increasingly clogged with speculative building which John Stow was lamenting even in 1599, and which over the centuries would not stop until it reached the wilds of Enfield and Essex.

The Curtain Theatre (centre, with flag flying)—from "a view of the Cittye of London from the North", C. 1600.

Yet it was here, in this unpromising fetid suburb, an arrow's flight from Leadenhall and a stone's throw from the windmills on what are now the hills of Angel Islington, that Elizabethan theatre effectively began. To supplement the inn yards that had since the 1570's proved popular venues for dramatic entertainments, the Theatre was built by Richard Burbage's father James, and became within a decade or so the vortex of a remarkable group of talents. Christopher Marlowe lived not far away, in slightly more

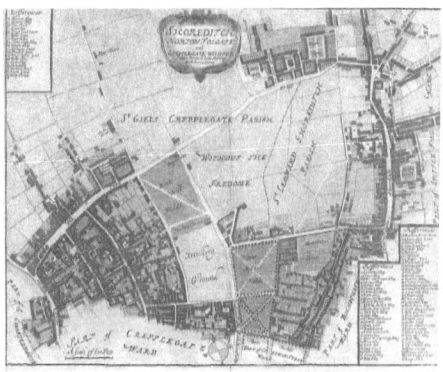

John Stow's map of Shoreditch & Norton Folgate, 1598.

Detail from "The View of the Cittye of London from the North towards the South", an engraving by Abram Booth, c. 1599, including a view of the Theatre.

And Curtain Road, Shoreditch today, looking south from the junction with Old Street. The 'Gherkin' is just visible in the distance. Photo: Dr. Neil Clifton 2008.
geograph.org..uk

elegant Norton Folgate – now just north of Liverpool Street Station - but let's face it, not much in London was really *elegant* then, except the palaces and Inns of Court. Broad Bishopsgate with its inns and its churches and its gentlemen's lodging houses petered out into rows of rude cottages, stinking streams, ditches, wild dogs, prostitutes - and the first public theatre in the Western world since ancient Greece.

Before setting off on the long journey to Stratford it would benefit the time-travelling explorer to prowl - Elizabethan A-Z in hand - the streets of Shakespeare's early neighbourhood in order to soak up the environment of his

5

twenties, to try to seek out and pinpoint the precise locations of his early workplaces, The Theatre, and the Curtain; the first built by James Burbage in the 1570's, the Curtain not long afterwards. It was in one of these venues that Shakespeare first stepped on stage and uttered his first words as an actor. Was anything left of them? Was it possible to discover anything remaining also of Shakespeare's lodging-house in St. Helen's, or the actor's hostel he probably stayed in at Holywell Lane?

In 1596 – the year I had chosen to recreate his journey - he was living in St. Helen's ward, about fifteen minutes walk from the theatres. This pattern of taking lodgings close to his workplaces indicates a daily necessity to actually be present during rehearsal and performance – this was no sit-at-home writer who sent his manuscripts in and moved on to the next piece. The fact that Shakespeare deliberately chose to live close to each theatre in which his plays were being produced is a strong indication that he was not only chief writer for the company, and actor, but also the director. Rehearsals took place in the mornings, so a short walk from home to work was vital.

The road-plan of sixteenth century London largely remains, though the buildings at the street's edges are changed, utterly changed...

Even in 1598 the great chronicler of London life and topography John Stow was mourning the passing of the semi-rustic idyll his childhood in the City had been. He describes the neighbourhood where Shakespeare first stayed when he moved to London from Stratford thus: "Hog Lane... within these forty years, had on both sides, fair hedgerows of elm trees, with bridges and easy stiles to pass over into the pleasant fields, very commodious for the citizens therein to walk, shoot and to otherwise recreate and refresh their dulled spirits in the sweet and wholesome air, which is now within a few yards made a continual building throughout... and the fields on either side be turned into garden plots... bowling alleys and such like." Hog Lane, now Worship Street, crossed Bishopsgate and would have been well-known to Shakespeare as he walked to and from work either at the Curtain or the Theatre. What is remarkable about this passage is that even in 1598 Stow refers to the need of the urban English citizen to escape from the stifling of his city surroundings and breathe "sweet and wholesome air."

Bishopsgate Street Ward in the City of London surveyed and published in 1720. Cartographer, Richard Blome; Surveyor, John Stow.

According to the tax records Shakespeare lived right next to St. Helen's Church from the early 1590's to around 1597.

St. Helen's lies just off Bishopsgate Road - but trying to locate it is an epic journey in itself, such is the looming grandeur and brutalism of the office buildings that have risen up on either side of this highway in the twentieth century. Old buildings have either been demolished or have slunk back, defeated, into the shadows, hidden away like embarrassing old demented relatives.

At last, I find the building that was Shakespeare's local church for his first seven or eight years in London...

St. Helen's Church, Bishopsgate. Shakespeare lived in St. Helen's ward from 1592-1598. Photo: Christine Matthews 2009.

Passing beneath the office-arch one emerges into an oasis of cool, religious space. I am in a courtyard. Quietude encloses me. I have gone back in time. A stooping plane tree trembles in the breeze. Children are playing in its shadow. The air is full of their timeless cries. Their parents are still meandering out of the church doorway, chattering politely to the vicar. A service has clearly just finished.

St. Helen's has a quiet, brooding Portland stone grandeur, a patina of mottled dark green moss dappling its broad smooth walls. Above the lintel on the right-hand entrance to the church is a modern inscription in white stone, which could apply to the Bard himself: *"Heaven and earth will pass away, but my words will never pass away."*

A converted monastic property, victim of Henry VIII's Dissolution, it was one of two fine buildings that Shakespeare's lodgings overlooked – the other being Crosby Hall, former home of Richard of Gloucester. The playwright wrote "Richard III" whilst lodging here, and set several scenes in Crosby Hall, erroneously but from sheer poetic licence.

The church was near to the Leather-seller's Hall and was frequented by wealthy merchants, including a Mercer (cloth trader) called Sir John "Rich" Spencer, who became Lord Mayor in 1594. Operating as a moneylender, Spencer may have been the origin of the line "You owe me ten shillings, say the bells of St. Helen's," – or maybe the area itself around the church was a locality known for usury. Shakespeare himself practised money-lending, as well as his father John who in 1570 was accused in the Exchequer Court of Usury for charging 20% and 25%. Did William move to St. Helen's because it was a place familiar to him, perhaps through visiting it with his father? – who, as a glove-maker, may have made a business trip or more to Leather-Sellers Hall next door to purchase the raw material of his trade and practice a bit of money-lending on the side? Perhaps the very lodging-house Shakespeare stayed in was obtained through a personal business contact of his Father's.

9

The Crosby Hall, next door to Shakespeare's lodgings in Bishopsgate, and former home of Richard of Gloucester. T.H. Shepherd 1830.

The actual site of Shakespeare's lodgings is a building that escapes anyone's descriptive powers because of its similarity to a million other structures – suffice to say it is gigantic, utilitarian, made of steel glass and concrete, and it is an upstanding rectangle.

That is all. There is no humanity in it; there are no decorative surfaces. There is no spirit in it. Its message to us is stark and cold - *inside here work is done and money is made.* In short, it is death itself.

And yet… if the house Shakespeare lived in were still here would it have been very different? Inside, work was certainly done and money made. But its stone would have been local, its beams would probably have been signed by the builder; its walls would probably have been painted with scenes of classical mythology or history. In short, it would have had a good few elements of *benign spirit.*

This dull expression of 1980's boredom is instantly beaten into defeat by the portly blue wonderment of the Skansk building looming fifty feet away; swollen, becalmed, confident, azure and coned, settled like a portly 1950s rocket-ship.

So here Shakespeare spent the first eight years or so of his life in London. From humble beginnings as a novice actor he rose to become not merely the greatest writer of his age, but probably for all time. And it is from here that every morning he would have left his lodgings after breakfast and walked to work up Bishopsgate Street to Shoreditch.

Before striking up Bishopsgate Street to follow his route to work I take a brief detour to look at Shakespeare's later stomping ground, the area around what is now the Barbican, to see if anything remains there of his Jacobean life.

I am sorely chastened. For if Shakespeare's Bishopsgate is difficult to descry, then recreating the neighbourhood he moved to later on in his career, around 1607 - when he lodged with the Mountjoy family on the corner of Silver Street and Monkswell Street not far from London Wall - is virtually impossible.

Leatherseller's Hall, near his lodgings, and which the playwright probably visited with his glove-maker father. Engraving 1799 by James Pellor Malcom.

11

Here one has to smash down whole vertical acres of steel and glass to travel back in time, such is the looming brutalism of the Barbican whose stairways in the sky crisscross London Wall like some 1950s illustration of a city of the future.

Nothing Elizabethan there, save once again the churches... An open space, however, is still an open space of sorts: Moorfields, where women dried clothes and bands of marching men once trained – *"is this Moorfields to muster in?"* complains a porter in "Henry VIII," grumbling at the stink, holding his nose and groaning at the "melancholy of Moorditch," – is now Finsbury Circus, prim with banks and insurance companies.

Abandon the Barbican, walk back east along the broad traffic-grinding highway of London Wall and Wormwood Street to Bishopsgate, past gleaming office buildings, the gigantic palaces of the fabulously wealthy lining the route where once stood the London Wall which skirted and protected the City in a semi-circular arc from Thames to Thames again; now smoothed down and broken to a series of odd shapeless rubble-heaps hidden behind skyscrapers: companies with names like *Schneitzer-Curling Holdings plc* and *Ballings Assurance*. Foyers the size of Renaissance Cathedrals, foliage so fecund it could fill a provincial arboretum; fountains splashing crystal waters on rose-coloured Tuscan marble, glass lifts rising up through the spine of the building like some fulfilment of a nineteen-fifties science fiction film.

Shakespeare's route to work would have taken him up Bishopsgate to Shoreditch High Street. The Inns that once used to line Bishopsgate were also Shakespeare's regular workplaces, as they often served as venues for the blossoming drama of the age.

Shoreditch High Street looking north: Shakespeare's route to work each morning. Photo: Stacey Harris 2010.

Holywell Lane, the site of the actor's lodging house where Shakespeare lived when he first moved to London in the late 1580's.

13

Do any of the great Inns remain? In Shakespeare's day the area boasted dozens, lasting centuries until modern developers bulldozed them for insurance companies. They had names like the Dolphin, the White Hart, the Black Bull, the Bell, the Cross Keys, the Vine, the Peahen, the Four Swans, the White Horse, the Wrestlers, the Saracen's Head, the Angel – and further East, just inside the city wall in Newgate Street, the Bel Savage. They are noteworthy in that most of them were probable venues for fit-up plays where of an evening dozens of theatricals would swarm into the yard, set up a stage, and to the half-swilled ale-lifting crowds, add poetry to the warm twilit air. In one of them Shakespeare himself probably gave an early performance as an actor – almost certainly the Cross Keys.

Optimistically I cross over Bishopsgate to the White Hart. Inside, throngs of shell-suited and pin-striped lads watch Sky TV on a screen so big their heads move from side to side as though they're watching a tennis match at Wimbledon.

I go outside to see if anything of an ancient Tudor Yard remains behind. I pass beneath a dark dripping archway. Sadly the remnant of the yard behind the pub is now bricked in and tiny. Big green plastic bins are stacked where the stage was. No galleries.

So, there are no Elizabethan Inns left in Bishopsgate. In fact, the only inn left in London still intact, with its galleries still overlooking the courtyard, is the George in Southwark, where Chaucer's pilgrims gathered pre-pilgrimage and Pickwick's gang met to set off on their summer, sunny jaunt.

On his way to work Shakespeare would have passed the Bedlam Hospital, where now stands Liverpool Street Station. Past Hog Lane, and he was in theatreland. Here he began his career, either as an actor or, as tradition states, a holder of horses. As I walk and attempt to scan the roads and buildings for any remnant of the Tudor Age, I conclude that little has survived of the Elizabethan city save for the road-plan itself, and the churches.

The road-plan is nevertheless crucial - and the street-names themselves provide a sort of linguistic archaeology: Spital Alley, Fleur de Lis Street; narrow alleyways which disappear into darkness on the right hand side of Bishopsgate Street as you walk north – Spital Alley with its soot-black early seventeenth century house with barred windows, birthplace of the Mother of John Wesley in 1669; and Fleur de Lis Street - dark, silent and cobbled, with its black Victorian lamp-posts arranged like a neat parade of extremely slender uniformed policemen. Here, in these nooks and crannies, one can derive a whiff of the Tudor age.

So the street-plan remains, and I guess the actual character of the area hasn't changed that much. As anyone who knows London will tell you, the city alters its character with every street you cross. Once you get north of Liverpool Street Station with its residual glamour of business travel and the glow of rich shops and giant corporations of the City with their gigantic foyers and their transparent lifts, there is a sense that the money hasn't quite reached this far. Shoreditches' streets are shabbier, the shops rougher, less expensive. It must always have been like this, even in Shakespeare's day.

It now seems a place to pass through rather than a settled community; such is the power of a traffic routeway to dominate an area's character. Stray from the main road away from the grinding headache of cars and you find yourself in dead alleyways with weeds sprouting. Behind the stiff and grubby façade of the street frontage, buildings lie broken, like lego houses built by children who've become bored and wandered off...

15

In the 1590's there was an iron foundry just beyond Bishopsgate, belching out industrial fumes and waste – and here, remarkably, four hundred years later in Shoreditch High Street, there is still a Wells Commercial Iron works, the signage clearly Victorian in style but nevertheless perhaps indicative of its earlier, Tudor forefather. In Curtain Road I pause opposite a 1960's office block. It looks empty, with those dull strips of dusty cream vertical blinds at the windows, turned inwards. Some planning official in the 60's must have remembered or found out that the area was renowned in the olden days for certain theatrical activity – for the building is called "Burbage House."

Remarkably, Holywell Lane, where stood the actor's lodging-houses Shakespeare may have stayed in on his arrival, is still there. It is now an empty, forgotten pathway of slug-brown cobbles and barbed wire twisting under a black railway arch. Yet it still connects Shoreditch High Street with Curtain Road. I try to hear the laughter and carousing of a dozen Elizabethan actors as they stumble home in their cups after a memorable performance of *Titus Andronicus*. The whole length of the byway is bisected by the soot-caked bulk of a nineteenth century railway bridge; on one side, a fenced off car-park with one of those huge yellow NCP signs. I try to imagine what it was like in Shakespeare's day. A windmill once stood across the road, and broad tenters' fields where women stretched out large cloths, pegging them in the ground to dry out in the sun.

Now dusty office-blocks blot out the sky.

And what of the Theatre, Shakespeare's first London workplace? After much retracing of steps, A-Z in hand, I manage to pinpoint its precise location... 86-90 Curtain Road.

And here it is...

City Dry Cleaners, Mediterranean Brunch Deli, and Foxton's Estate Agents.

I stare deep through the windowpanes of the shops, into the heart of an impenetrable darkness. Is there a statue of James Burbage? A neat heritage-lottery financed arrangement of cobbled courtyard, coffee bar, information centre and gift-shoppe? No. But there is a fine stone plaque. I linger awhile, trying to travel back in time mentally and to see, with half-closed eyes, Richard Burbage arriving for work, Shakespeare handing in his latest batch of large foolscap pages…

My reflection stares back at me. Perhaps this is an apt metaphor for anyone's quest who attempts to solve the "enigma" of Shakespeare? Do they end up staring at themselves?

Woken by traffic noise, my footsteps take me slowly back to Shakespeare's lodgings in St. Helen's; at least one can walk the actual alleyway along which he must have embarked on the first few steps of his journey – Winding Lane. Back to the Skansk Gherkin, swollen in plump proud blue shade, a building of power and beauty. But for our purposes of time travel let us now smash it down and rebuild the crooked wattle-and-daub lodging-house with dark narrow stairway smelling of tallow and oak, the casement windows slightly ajar for it is a balmy August morning, the crier's voices in the streets: Shakespeare upstairs stirring on his goose-feather or sacking mattress…

What of his waking? What was he thinking and feeling on this summer morning of August 1st 1596? He was the first writer in the history of the world to give his characters an interior life. What of his interior life as he woke?

St. Ethelburga, Bishopsgate. Photo: ChrisO 2004.

CHAPTER TWO

SICK WITH THE WORKING OF MY
THOUGHTS: SETTING OFF

An untrammelled washing-machine chaos of worry, reassurance, patchwork formulation of plans for the day, and that clockwork nag, nag, nag of a voice inside us that we sometimes like and sometimes hate and never discover from where it comes: *"I am sick with the working of my thoughts..."* This, if Shakespeare was anything like the rest of us, was his consciousness as he stirred on the morning of his embarkation.

He rises. He stumbles over in his nightgown to his washstand. Let's hear the playful splash of the playwright's water as he freshens his face – dipping his ink-stained hands in the large white bowl... water brought up to him by a servant of the house while he slept, bought from a water-carrier at the front door that very morning.

For all across the City were conduits – channels and outlets and pumps for the spring water that gushed from underneath London's streets. The citizens were allowed to use this water freely, the poorer having to traipse themselves to the conduits, the financially able buying it from carriers who'd stalk the streets with their hulking wooden cans of the precious cool stream water shouting their wares.

London then, of course, was powered by wind and water. Mills graced the banks of the city's many rivers and streams - the Walbrook, the Fleet, the Tyburn – and domestic water-supply itself ran through pipes from these tributaries and the Thames itself to the conduits dotted about the city; chiefly in Cheapside and Bishopsgate itself. The water would be carried in large wooden cans, like milkchurns.

As an aspiring gentleman, Shakespeare would have had his water brought upstairs to his room for his morning ablutions.

Let us put his washstand at his window looking north.

Shakespeare's view as he looked out of his window was dominated, of course, by St. Helen's – principally the Chapel of Our Lady.

Below him he would have seen a few tradesmen in Winding-Lane, a water-carrier pushing a wooden container on a small handcart, apprentices on their way to work. Beyond that – depending on how high up he was – he could have seen the fields of Moorfields with the great stretched-out swathes of drying cloths – and further, the bristling windmills on the slopes of what is now the Angel Islington.

From three floors below him, the sounds of breakfast waft – the chatter of tradesmen at the front door, the dull clunk of another water-can slammed down on the doorstep. The first meal would have been bought from the street-traders along with the water. Fresh bread would have been bought from a baker carrying loaves in a tray along the flagstones of Winding Lane, and butter maybe, and sage. Beer would have been in the house.

A repast of butter, bread, sage and beer would have been brought up to Shakespeare to his room – or he would have eaten it downstairs. For Elizabethans there were two main cooked meals of the day – the principal one being at eleven o'clock to twelve noon when they'd sit down to four or more courses of meat and fish and fruit tarts. Then dinner at six or seven – the same, only more. Fruit and sweets would have been eaten between each course, not just at the end. But Shakespeare's breakfast would have been quite simple – bread and beer. Or maybe, as he was due to set off on a long journey and was perhaps planning lunch for around twelve-thirty or one o'clock, he had a larger meal – perhaps Christmas pie.

Last night he'd been packing. One can smell the candle-smoke in his room, hear the scratch of his quill as he sent word to his wife to expect him in three days, the creak of his chair as he leant back…

Slowly, methodically, Shakespeare washes and combs his beard.

What is his room like?

Elizabethan bedroom. Slightly grander probably than Shakespeare's lodgings, this interior nevertheless gives an idea of his domicility in Bishopsgate and, later, Moorgate.

22

His walls are pale wattle and daub, the colour of local earth. These are quite handsome rooms, for although most of his money is spent in his home town of Stratford, his life in London is not Spartan. There is certainly a desk. Shakespeare spent many hours at home writing. When invited out he would often refuse, making the excuse that he had toothache.

As he washes, what does he hear, smell?

The noise would have been great: though not, I suspect, as pervasive as it is now, not as "background." It would have been piecemeal, local, not universal like modern traffic. Yes, the clatter of cart on the hard limestone highways, and yes, the stink of waste from the ditches – Houndsditch is, after all, named after the dogs that quite plainly fouled its banks and slopes – mortally offending in the summer when there was little running water. A summer breeze would have wafted this stench to Shakespeare as he dried his face at the open window. Brick and lime kilns beyond Bishopsgate added to the sour scent with their attendant belching of smoke. Large gun-foundries lay just beyond Houndsditch, contributing their din and fumes. But none of the grinding ache of internal combustion engine, the exhausting sick petrol dizzy smell fugging the broad roads. From his window he probably could see the row of windmills on the horizon on top of the rubbish tips of Finsbury fields.

What was he feeling? Relaxed? He was, after all, about to go on holiday: that broad, open, blue-sky feeling, no more writing for a few weeks, seeing his children again, his wife…

Bad news, however, may have reached him a few days earlier - in the summer of 1596 his boy Hamnet had fallen ill. As he finished his packing was he troubled by a tug and wrench of anxiety for his only son?

23

My surmise is that Shakespeare's feeling about having to return once or twice a year to his Stratford home and family was ambiguous. I suspect that the double-life he led – that of a famous playwright whose work led him to rub shoulders with the leading noblemen and women of the day, as well as intellectuals, writers, artists, and political supremos; and that of a stolid country gentleman slowly and patiently building up his portfolio of land and property whilst rubbing shoulders with plain Midlands folk whose talk would have been of horses, grain prices, local affairs - led to a double-feeling. Whilst in Stratford I'm guessing Shakespeare had occasional pangs of gentle scorn for the dullness of his peers, combined with a dash of regret that he wasn't returning to the cut and thrust of city life for another few weeks, with its intrigue, its exciting personalities, its cutting-edge swiftness and vividness.

And yet, on balance... I think the playwright preferred Stratford. He made his home there, he retired there... he clearly had great affection for the market town with its long summer days, its wildnesses in the fields and meadows, its flowers (in particular its flowers, the names of which pockmark the plays with frequency). He filled his plays with Stratford names. His life's work glows with love for his county. There are so many Warwickshire-sourced elements in the plays that they alone stand as a confident and invincible rebuttal to the ludicrous fantasies of the anti-Stratfordians.

So let us give to him a lightness of heart as he stands at his window looking out onto the blue, the deep blue summer sky, above the crooked brown rooftops.

More of his room: as we are setting this journey in 1596 he would have been rising but not yet rich – his great Jacobean work was to come. He was making money but not yet a millionaire – indeed, we must remember that while he was living in the St. Helen's ward he had to evade his taxes, so he can't have been rolling in it. It was probably the most exciting time of his life – that time of your life when you have extricated yourself from that unfocussed, confusing and un-moneyed state of your early twenties: you can see the road ahead, you are aware of your talents, you have started to make money, and you can sense with growing momentum that where you want to go and what you want to do *will actually happen.*

So, at this point in his career, his room would have been clean and large but not lavish or luxurious. The walls as aforementioned would have been wattle and daub but the oak beams not black nor the plaster in between whitened with gypsum. The oak would have been a beautiful pale brown, the walls perhaps coloured by local earth.

Depending on how prosperous the house was there may have been wall-paintings, or painted wall-cloths; depictions of classical mythology maybe, or lutenists, or flowers, or biblical scenes.

His personal property in London was sparse – it was valued by tax collectors at five pounds. He lived in a succession of cheaply rented rooms in rough areas – Shoreditch, Bishopsgate, Bankside. This was not a man dedicated to leading an extravagant life in London – this was a man devoted to making money for his family in Warwickshire; his family including his Father, whose personal finances had collapsed at the end of the 1570's. Indeed, I strongly suspect that William kept his father for the rest of his life, which may have been one of the driving-forces of his ambition.

A desk, naturally. Shakespeare was at home, often, obviously – his work-rate and productivity scarcely indicates a hectic social life. According to Aubrey, he seldom went out – when invited by his friends he "...writ that he was in paine," ie. replied that he had toothache. Aubrey knew Christopher Beeston's son, Beeston having

Shakespeare's kitchen/dining room. "Kitchen at the Old King Street Bakery," by Frederick McCubbin 1884.

worked with the playwright, so this is an anecdote from life. When asked what made a great writer, James Joyce thought for a moment, then replied: "well, the most important thing is, you have to dine alone, at home, often."

Shakespeare must have dined at home alone often. He swam in an ocean of imagination for most of his waking life, detached from reality. Perhaps that explains his almost ambiguous attitude to the artificiality of the theatrical world; a feeling maybe of slight regret about dwelling in such unreality – in the Tempest he gets Prospero to break his staff and abjure the "rough magic." Maybe by 1610 or so he had had enough of the crazy world of making things up – he wanted the calm, clear rational, realm of the businessman

26

and country gentleman. So he took off to Stratford, and never came back.

He dresses.

According to the Chandos portrait – if indeed it is of him – then Shakespeare was a rather casual dresser. The loose collar and earring give the playwright a rather bohemian and somewhat louche image, quite unlike the formal and stuffy apparel of the Stratford monument where he resembles nothing less than a provincial burgher – which of course in his home town of Stratford he was.

A ruff, naturally, a shirt, and a doublet over the shirt buttoned with very small buttons either made of jewels or - more probably for a thrifty writer - wood. The doublet had a short, stiffened skirt from the waist covering the row of holes on to which the breeches were tied. No peasecod, not for travel. Around the waist was a girdle, made for carrying the tools of one's trade such as pen and inkhorn. Whether he wore his tools for his journey is not known, but unlikely. Over the doublet he put his jerkin; for working men they were common leather, for Shakespeare probably Spanish.

For travel he would then have donned his cloak. He probably had two – an ankle-length thick felt gabardine for Winter journeys, waist-length for clement trips: today in August 1596 then he shoulders his mid-length cloak and ties it loosely round his neck. On the legs, breeches, ending either above or below the knee; stockings, either silk or wool. As he was riding he may have gartered them, so as not to resemble Hamlet whose stockings "were foul, ungartered, and down-gyved to the ankle." But as he probably wore boots for the journey, the gartering was perhaps unnecessary; indeed, given his famous satirising of the practice in Malovolio, I do not see Shakespeare ever gartering his legs. It smacks of fussiness, pedantry, and lack of manliness.

Finally, strong leather boots for the rough country roads. In 1600, boots deliberately crafted for both the left and right foot had just begun to be made; before that date they were identical. So Shakespeare perhaps had no opportunity to take advantage of the novel style of footwear and have an easier time of it as he hauled his boots on.

Shakespeare's lodging house in Bishopsgate would not have looked dissimilar to this timbered house in Grub Street. (From "Elizabethan People," Henry Thew Stevenson, 1912.)

The boy clatters down the wooden stairs. He is carrying the playwright's bags for the horses' panniers. Following him down Shakespeare says goodbye to the housekeeper, or the family who own the lodgings. Maybe holding on to his own money-bags, he lets the boy carry two bags of apparel: writing material, gifts for his children, maybe the odd book or two - then steps out the front door onto flagstones.

And they are still there, the very ones he stepped on, within the yard of St. Helens itself, though beyond that boundary there is nothing but tarmac, under an overshadowing acreage of steel, glass and concrete.

Shakespeare probably began his journey home from the Bell Inn on Carter Lane just south of St. Paul's Cathedral, hiring a gelding from one William Greenaway. Why Greenaway? Because he was Stratford-upon-Avon's chief carrier, having plied the route between his home town and London since 1581. The Greenaways were close neighbours of the Shakespeare's in Henley Street. Letters and goods were transported to and fro by Greenaway.

So he would have walked down Bishopsgate, then probably down Threadneedle Street. The view that met Shakespeare as he left his lodging-house was the noble, pargeted door of St. Helen's Church. He would have turned left, then, up Winding Lane, his boy or man following with his bags; and on to Bishopsgate Street…

The houses in these back-streets, off the main thoroughfares, were good old wattle and daub, the main buildings in the wider streets being stone. But the wattle-and-daub houses would not have been the fashionable and pretty white which we are accustomed to – they would either have been utterly uncoloured – a kind of beige-brown, or a more pleasing rough ochre.

And they were tall – many comprising four floors. So this narrow street would have been shady. Winding Lane is still shady, but not from wattle and daub houses – rather with office blocks.

29

As I leave, the children are still playing noisily in the church courtyard in the dappled sunshine of the huge plane tree, much as they might have done four hundred years earlier.

As he stepped out of the mouth of Winding Lane into the hard bright sunshine of an August Bishopsgate Street, Shakespeare would at once have found himself in a throng - even in early morning the streets would have been packed.

Stow laments the crowding of the thoroughfares in London, complaining of the clamour and the din; indeed much of Stow's work is a lament – even in 1590 he was complaining of the buildings being thrown up all along Bishopsgate right up to Shoreditch, ruining his memory of the sweet-smelling fields where, no doubt, as a boy he ran and played and made merry. What would Stow make of it now, a city that reaches north to Enfield, West to Northolt, South to Penge and East to Epping?

And so, out into the world from the realm of his imagination. The feeling of coming out of a cinema, maybe, into pitiless light, after that temporary loss of self in the wonder of romance or adventure. The cruel dullness of reality hits hard. And what of his son Hamnet, whose illness his wife has recently informed him of? Was Shakespeare's heart heavy as he set off on his homeward journey? What lies ahead of him? Grief, joy, a sick son, a journey deep into the labyrinth of his own mind as his beast winds its way into the heart of England?

He grits his teeth and steps out into Bishopsgate, into the sun, into the river of life, into the hell of other people, into the swarm of men.

The alleyway of Great St. Helen's Shakespeare walked along on leaving his lodgings. Photo: Henry Dixon, 1870's.

.... and the same view four hundred years later.
Photo: British Library.

CHAPTER THREE

MY GRIEF LIES ONWARDS:
BISHOPSGATE TO CARTER LANE

In Elizabethan times long pack-trains of horses and mules threaded their way through the streets and lanes of London carrying produce, building materials and meat through Ludgate or Newgate to Oxford, through Bishopsgate to Suffolk and Norfolk, across London Bridge to Kent and Sussex, and through Aldgate to Essex. Many of the main streets were paved, so the air would have been ringing all day with the clatter of hoof on limestone.

It was probably with one of these trading convoys that the playwright travelled, or indeed with William Greenaway if the carrier was going back to Stratford.

Shakespeare's fellow Warwickshireman Greenaway used to carry local goods from his home-town such as skins, cheeses, gloves, etc. (gloves made, perhaps, by the playwright's father himself) as well as mail, then on the return journey he would supply the Stratford citizens with produce from

London - more exotic stuff from afar, like oranges, pepper, sugar, raisins and limes.

It was dangerous to travel alone, especially if carrying money, as Shakespeare probably was. In the year following this journey, 1597, the playwright would purchase New Place in Stratford for £60.00 — a fortune which probably travelled with him in leather bags, protected by two armed henchmen.

Two henchmen figure often in Shakespeare's plays, and they are usually very well drawn — almost excessively so for their length of time on-stage. Is it perhaps a fancy to suggest that the writer's annual or bi-annual journey in the company of two such professional guards may have been the inspiration for these memorable duos?

At the top of Winding Lane, then, with Crosby Hall on his left, Shakespeare would have turned left and headed for a few brief steps down Bishopsgate Street on his way to Carter Lane south of St. Pauls. At this southern end of Bishopsgate Street were the main fish, herb and meat markets of the district, with their attendant fragrances. Also, the odd beggar, perhaps, capitalising on the nearby Bedlam just a few yards north beyond the city wall

Bethlehem Hospital, founded in 1247, would have been very familiar to Shakespeare, as he would have passed it as he walked to and fro on his way to work at either the Curtain or the Theatre. Fake insanity was a popular ploy amongst itinerants, and surely we have a fine example of Shakespeare writing from life when we see Edgar in King Lear metamorphose into poor "Tom o' Bedlam" - the nickname for the perpetrators of counterfeit madness, possessed as he was with the spirits of Mohad and Flibertigibbet. Was the playwright remembering the numerous imitation lunatics he must have stepped over on the pavement during his daily journey to and from work throughout the 1590's? And the feigned madness of Hamlet – was that fleshed out with snatches of overheard garbled monologue from the counterfeit maniacs who paraded Bishopsgate Street from dawn to dusk?

The Bethlehem Hospital is now the Great Eastern Hotel, right next to Liverpool Street Station. So Shakespeare would have crossed over Bishopsgate Street - (paved, as were several of the main arteries of London with good "flint and limestone," as was noted by a foreign traveller) - thronging as it was with pack animals, wagons and crowds - and begun threading his way through the jostling merchants in their long fur-trimmed gowns and flat woollen caps on their way to the docks and quays to oversee their goods unloaded by large cranes mounted on axles at Fish wharf, Timberhithe, Salt Wharf, or Hay Wharf…

Junction of Bishopsgate & Threadneedle Street, site of St. Martin's Outwich church which Shakespeare would have passed. Photo: Basher Eyre, 2008.

... and then passed over into Threadneedle Street, or "three needle street" as it was probably then called, with the church of St. Martin's Outwich and its burial ground (demolished in 1874) on his left as he stepped onto the kerb. To his right on the corner of Bishopsgate Street he would have seen the Church of St. Botolph's – an older building than the present 1725 version: in Shakespeare's was baptised his erstwhile colleague, the Elizabethan matinee idol and first theatre millionaire of the age, Edward Alleyn.

Former site of Bartholemew-by-the-Exchange, Threadneedle Street. Photo: Basher Eyre 2008.

Here, the view to my right as I cross the road, if I was the Bard, would have been dominated by the huge Bishops' Gate.

It must be remembered that the Gates of London – Aldgate, Cripplegate, Ludgate, Newgate etc. – were not simply gates as we know them but rather gigantic fortress-like buildings, edifices housing dozens of guards, bailiffs, and even, in the case of Newgate, prisoners: indeed, Newgate would outlive the demolition of Londons' gates and continue as a penal complex.

The only thing remaining now of Bishopsgate itself – the actual gate – is a rather surreal Bishop's mitre set in the roughened concrete corner of a 1970's office block.

Threadneedle Street was also called "Needler's Lane," from it being the ancient site of the Merchant Taylor's Guild; this road was a fine route to Poultry and the broad highway now known as Cheapside. The grand Taylor's Hall would have been on his left, and further down on the other side of the road, the church of St. Anthony. Shakespeare would have felt at home passing the Skinner's and the Tailor's shops on this street, his father having practiced the same profession, being a glove-maker.

One thing that strikes me about Threadneedle Street today is how narrow it is. Flanked by banks galore, of course, the frontages of pale regency stone an odd contrast with the garish adverts in their windows of smiling people eager to give us money: *"We can lend you anything for anything!"*- a Holmes Health Club now jostling with the National Bank of Italy, while a huge new office development shooting up on the side of Throgmorton Street threatens to force the gentler, more quirky Victorian side of the road into cowering defeat: the Draper's Hall, with its curlicued statues of giants holding up the earth, and its Lions and Unicorns, looking sad and defeated below the looming viciousness of blank euro-money architecture; *("our company has a property portfolio of eight billion...")*

Quaint origins still shine through the street-names, however: Finch Lane on the left, though no birdsong now. Needles have, of course, been long ago cast aside for abacus's, and later, computers. I can find no lingering echo of its clothes-making heritage at all, but... just as I reach

Cheapside, I spot the "Savoy Taylor's Guild," – realising a few moments later that it's just a branch of Moss Bros.

Shakespeare would have passed the beautiful church of St. Bartholemew by the Exchange, which lay on the right side of Three Needle Street about half way down. It was destroyed by the Great Fire of London, rebuilt by Wren in 1666 – only to be demolished by the Victorian money-men in 1841.

As he approached Poultry the first sight that would have met his eyes is the huge Stocks (Market)– the origin, of course, of the "Stock-market," not the later eighteenth century financial term.

More banks and building societies – Alliance and Liecester, Bradford and Bingley… Bucklersbury Passage where lived a friend of Shakespeare, John Sadler, a fellow-Stratfordian who'd moved to London around the same time as he and who rose to become a prosperous grocer: (Falstaff mocks the fops who "smell like Bucklersbury in simple-time," simples being herbs for medicines). The place where the playwright's friend lived is now a giant rose-red corporation whose building has the imaginative name "Number One Poultry," site of the former Lorimer's Guild. Lorimers were the makers of spurs, bits and harnesses for horses.

Here, at the junction of Cornhill, Lombard Street and Threadneedle Street, was the great Conduit, and the entrance to broad, vibrant and colourful Cheapside.

The delightful Victorian antiquary Walter Thornbury describes the old London conduits as "pleasant gathering places for 'prentices, serving-men and serving girls – open-air parliaments of chatter, scandal, love-making and trade-talk. Here all day repaired the professional water-carriers, rough sturdy fellows like Ben Jonson's Cob, who were hired to supply the houses of the rich Goldsmiths of Chepe, and who, before Sir Hugh Middleton brought the New

River to London, were indispensable to the citizen's existence." So the conduits were the Elizabethan equivalent of today's office water-coolers, both functionally and socially. The New River was officially opened in 1613, so Shakespeare's was the last generation to rely solely on them.

Every city has its places of loiter and chat to which people drift and collect like iron filings to a magnet. Ned Ward in 1700 wrote that Cheapside Conduit was "palisaded with chimneysweepers' brooms, and surrounded by sweeps probably waiting to be hired, so that a countryman, seeing so many black attendants waiting at a stone hovel, took it to be one of old Nick's tenements." A hundred years after Shakespeare's morning walk on his way to Carter Lane, but I would place a hefty bet on the ancientness of the tradition, such do these habits linger in cities and towns. Walk the streets of London today and you will see cab-drivers parked up in neat black rows, chatting and smoking roll-ups in precisely the same spots as where their forefathers the carters lingered on a break. At the top of Carnaby Street at the junction of Great Marlborough Street you can see leather-clad clusters of motorcycle couriers accreting at various loitering-points waiting to be hired. So I would wager that in 1596 the playwright passed several mumbling sweeps lounging round the conduit as he strolled past.

For many centuries Cheapside could lay claim to being London's High Street, in the retail sense of the word. It was packed with taverns and shops of all descriptions, and was wide and spacious enough for huge Royal Tournaments. Some of the houses were five storeys high, and sixty three properties were owned by Goldsmiths. J.B. Black remarks that one of the great sights of London was "West Cheap with its far-famed Goldsmith's Row, noted for its glittering tower and its fountain that played continuously." ("Reign of Elizabeth," Oxford History of Britain).

Signs swaying in the summer breeze that Shakespeare would have seen as he passed down Cheapside were the Black Bear, the Acorn, the Three Wells, the Broad Arrow, the Holy Ghost, and the Black Boy. The names denoted the building, and not the trade carried out within. Goods were often sold outside the fronts of the premises, and not hidden away inside with elaborate window displays. So a market street would have smelt strongly with what was being sold – herbs, meat, fish.

Cheapside 1890. Library of Congress, Detroit Publishing Co.

41

Remnants of Cheapside's glorious retail past remain only in the language of the street-names: Ironmonger Lane, Honey Lane, Wood Street, Bread Street. Passing the Great Conduit on his right, situated as Poultry became Chepe proper, the playwright would then have moved down the pavement past, on his left, the church of St. Mary le Bow, famous now for its bells bestowing cockney identity on those babies born within their sound. Of warm red brick, the church - once a shining raiment of Wren's London - is pockmarked now and a little shabby, marked by the rain and snow of five hundred winters. In its garden is a statue of one of Shakespeare's contemporaries, someone he most certainly knew and probably met, being one of London's great celebrities of the age: Captain John Smith (1580-1631) founder of Jamestown, Virginia, and therefore one of those Voyaging Adventurers who came back to the city with stories of treasures and natives and strange creatures, inspiring a playwright perhaps to write the Tempest. Did Shakespeare meet Pocahontas, the Native American who became the toast of London society?

Falstaff of course haunted the inns and back-streets of Cheapside - the Piccadilly or the Soho of the age, with its drink, its voluptuous women and its chop-houses.

Across the road on the south-west corner of Wood Street lies a fragment of the churchyard of St. Peters, Cheap, destroyed by the Great Fire and not rebuilt – merely a few headstones leaning as though tired against the black railings, in which is set a strange figure of an old bearded man carrying a book and a key, a figure not unlike an idealised Shakespeare until I realise it must of course be St. Peter. Towering above is a broad-trunked rough-barked plane-tree, centuries-old and famous. Thornbury praises the tree as the provider of welcome refreshment to the weary businessman, giving him visions of faraway fields and hills, while Leigh Hunt referred to it as the only tree many London children knew as they grew up in the area around St. Paul's, after an even-more famous tree was felled in the churchyard. It's true there aren't many plane trees in the City proper — you have to go to the Regency and Victorian West End to see trees as part of the planned layout of the streets.

There was a pianoforte shop on the corner of Wood Street in the nineteenth century — it is now a Phones4U. The original lease of the shops directly below the tree forbade them to be extended any higher so as to keep the tree visible from the street — and now, centuries later, here they are, at the same height.

Cheapside now peters out at its western end into a vague broad grey traffic-route with one tarmac artery taking cars south down New Change and another channelling them West to Newgate Street: the only acknowledgement that people might actually want to walk somewhere being a double pelican crossing. Newgate leads straight across Holborn ("Old Bourne Bridge") and out West along "Bloomsbury High Street" and Oxford Street — but before escaping the City proper Shakespeare first had to make a diversion left towards Carter Lane, in order to obtain his mount.

In this year of 1596 he would have passed on his right the great Cross of Cheapside, one of several built by Edward III to mark the resting-places of his beloved wife Eleanor's coffin on its route from Lincoln to Westminster. This cross is a potent symbol of the religious tensions of the age. A grand and rather flamboyant depiction of the Virgin and Child, this expression of "idolatry" was subject to sporadic puritanical vandalism over the years — the head of the "popish" statues being removed, the gilt smashed, even the figure of the Child defaced. In 1595 it had only just been restored by Elizabeth when, a mere twelve days later, it was attacked yet again. As a local man Shakespeare would have seen or been aware of the tension, the passion and the violence this work of art inspired. He would have heard the news in the evening as he and his colleagues repaired to the Mermaid after a performance at the Bull in Bishopsgate – "cross torn down again."

On his way to Carter Lane he would have taken one of the lanes which branched south of Cheapside and past the back of St. Pauls - down Bread Street perhaps, Old Change Street or Friday Street. If he took Bread Street not only would he have been assailed by the rich warm fragrance of freshly cooked loaves, but also by the sight perhaps of John Milton's father, who would have been starting work in his scrivener's shop. Being of an allied trade to play-writing, Shakespeare probably knew him; as a masque writer, he most certainly did. Did he hire the future poet's father to write fair copies of his plays? We have no word, but it's possible. Shakespeare wrote out his "foul" papers, but to present it to the actors for rehearsal the manuscript would have been re-drafted by a professional scribe. Shakespeare was also an actor and director and producer, so would scarcely have had the time.

I like to think he turned left down Friday Street. Why? Because on Friday Street stood the legendary Mermaid tavern. He may have stopped off there to bid farewell to friends.

Founded, as tradition goes, by Walter Raleigh as a Club of writers, artists and intellectuals, the Mermaid became the social hub of the age: the place where the eminent minds of the era ate, drank, talked, and played – the haunt of Jonson, Drayton, Donne and Shakespeare himself, among many others. The ingredients of many of the greatest books and plays of the era doubtless were mixed within its walls; the wit-combat of Beatrice and Benedict, the dangerous heresy of Faustus, Raleigh's world history – all had their genesis in this memorable vortex. Memories of the place and its occasions were treasured: Shakespeare's younger friend and collaborator Francis Beaumont wrote:

What things have we seen,
Done, at the Mermaid? – heard words that have been
So nimble, and so full of subtle flame
As if everyone from which they came
Had meant to put his whole wit in a jest,
And had resolved to live a fool the rest of his dull life.

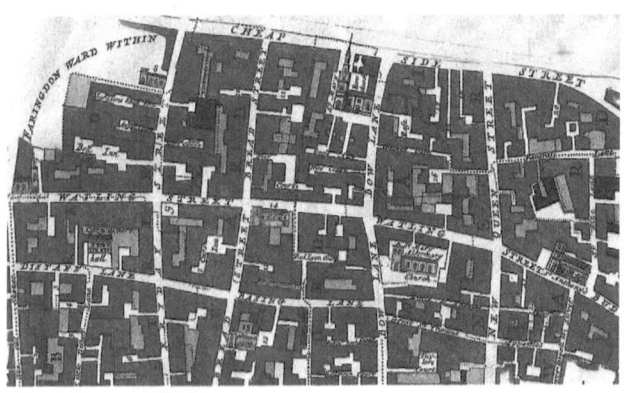

Stow's map of Cheapside & the streets radiating south
including St. Mary le Bow, Bread Street where Milton's
father worked as a scrivener, & Friday Street, home of the
Mermaid Tavern.

But where precisely was the Mermaid ? There are several references to the Mermaid Tavern across the centuries and each mention places it at a slightly different location; in

Friday Street, and on Cheapside itself. Were there several Mermaids? I think not. I believe that when writing of the famous tavern some writers were deriving their knowledge from hearsay and lazily wrote Cheapside when it probably should have been Friday Street.

Engraving of Old St Pauls Cathedral.

The area around St. Paul's Cathedral would have been familiar stomping ground of the playwright, given that it was the home of publishers, printers and booksellers. There is anecdotal evidence of the playwright being seen spending hours in various bookshops here; maybe in the shop of his old Stratford friend, the printer Richard Field, who could have lent him books.

The Cathedral was a hub of the social universe of London, *"a house of talking, of walking, of brawling, of minstrelsy, of hawks and of dogs."* Businessmen and traders, ruffians, beggars, booksellers and prostitutes – representatives of all strata of English society - all gathered inside and out, pursuing their needs. The middle aisle of the nave was the haunt of "idle gentlewomen" and rough "gallant gentlemen" who would meet to exchange "favours;" the tombs were used as counting tables for business transactions.

Outside in the yard was even noisier: horses and mules used the cathedral precincts as a short-cut, leading to "din and confusion," winding past the many rows of bookstalls where Shakespeare would doubtless have bought the numerous "merry books of Italy" that proved such valuable sources for his dramas.

Shakespeare, then, would have walked beneath the shadow of the huge cathedral and past the book-market, with maybe the odd word with a friend or acquaintance.

Today, the area immediately south of St. Paul's is given over completely to through-traffic heading West along Queen Victoria Street or Thames Street on its way to Blackfriars and the embankment. But clustering around Carter Lane there survives a network of old buildings and a warren of lanes and back-streets that is possibly one of the best preserved areas of Shakespeare's London.

As he made his way past St. Paul's, ahead of him would been Distaff Alley and Old Fish Street Hill. The land slopes quite dramatically here as it makes its way down to the riverbank thirty or forty yards away; bearing right, he would have reached Carter Lane.

Carter Lane still follows precisely the same path it did four hundred years ago. It is surprisingly narrow for a place known for traffic and the hiring of carriages. On the left is a modern office building – "Wren House" of course – but as you pass down the lane a network of alleyways and courts branch off on either side; alleys and courts the playwright would have passed – Addle Hill, Creed Lane, Wardrobe Place, Friar Street, Ireland Yard, Cobb's Court – the latter so narrow you'd have to pass down it sideways. Here, far more so than in the huge out-sized corporate City we've left behind, is a sizeable portion of the actual London Shakespeare knew.

Carter Lane, south of St. Paul's, where Shakespeare collected his horse from Richard Greenaway. Photo: Chris Downer 2008.

The reason of course for the area's successful preservation is the fact that for centuries it has been church land:

fragments of the old Blackfriars Dominican Priory still remain, its churchyard now reduced to two small square lunching areas for local office workers - but preserved nevertheless. Dissolved in 1538, its hall given over from devotional purposes to a more secular devotion – that of Shakespeare's greatest works, performed within Blackfriar's Theatre from 1601 – 1614. Here, somewhere, was Lear's voice first heard, and Prospero's, and Mark Antony's. Also in Blackfriars was the Royal Wardrobe, Master of the Revels, and various Court Treasurers. The King's Men's new theatre was in a hall in the former monastery's fratery, measuring 46 by 66 feet. Here the company took up their winter quarters, much to the chagrin of the neighbours who complained of the crowds that thronged the narrow streets from one o'clock to six at night.

*

Carter Lane is very old and probably dates from the 12th century, at that time being known as Shoemakers' Row. Its present name did not appear until the beginning of the 13th century when the Lane was divided into Great and Little Carter Lane. Inns and Taverns were at one time plentiful here: there was the Rising Sun, Saracen's Head, White Horse, the Bell, and others - in fact, one on almost every corner. Of these, the Rising Sun is the only one remaining. Occupying the west corner of Burgon Street, it faces Creed Lane, the passage up to Ludgate Hill, with a huge curved bow of wall like the bulwarks of a generously proportioned ship. It was about the most homely of the Carter Lane set; a tavern where the telephone operators of Faraday House mingled with the printers of Royle's next door. Its bar was a treasure of wooden panelling, etched mirrors, and varnished Lincrusta extending part way up the walls. From the upstairs

Playhouse Yard, site of Blackfriar's Theatre where Shakespeare staged his later plays from 1600 onwards. Photo: Basher Eyre, 2008.

restaurant a small, cosy, informal chop bar emitted the enticing aroma of simple, home cooking.

On the corner of Dean's Court is the old St Paul's Choir School dating from 1875, with its playground on the roof, now in the hands of the Youth Hostel Association. Still almost as fresh as the day it was stencilled is the Latin inscription on the frontage to the building - *"Nihi autrem arbrit glorian nisi in cruce domini nostri jesu Christi."*

Turning to the eastern end of Carter Lane, just past Dean's Court, is Bell Yard, at one time the alleyway leading to the Bell Inn. It was from this hostelry in 1598 that Richard Quyney sat down with quill in his hand and wrote to his 'loving good ffrend and contreyman Mr Willm Shackespere'. This is the only known surviving letter written to the playwright, a request for a loan - it is now preserved at Stratford-on-Avon. The inn has long gone but Bell Yard is still there, complete with its fading painted sign. However, a high wooden gate bars access.

A neighbour of Shakespeare's, John Sadler of Stratford – he of Bucklersbury - left his home town for London around the same time as the aspiring actor-playwright, and made the journey by "hiring a horse and joining himself to the carrier."

This would have been the principal mode of long-distance travel for both gentleman and one of more lowly status – the hiring of a horse from one of the carrying firms of the city.

In the sixteenth century all Government mail was carried by the official Post – horsemen engaged by the carriers who raced along the highways pell-mell at a speed that would render the commentators at Aintree falsetto in their paroxysms. In 1517, a Governor of the King's Post was appointed, and by 1572 when Thomas Randolph was appointed Master of the Posts, the postal service was official and permanent. But this was purely for official mail – private communication was one's own affair. This state-sponsored system, however, established a network and an industry that seeped into the private sector. For as the stabling and the inns grew up to support the transport of government correspondence and officials, then it was a natural progression, for purely commercial reasons if nothing else, to support the growing need for ordinary people to travel between town and city.

The speed of these couriers was famous – so much so that Shakespeare uses their rapidity as a metaphor on numerous occasions in his plays: in King Lear he describes "A reeking post, Stewd in his haste, half-breathless, panting forth from Goneril his mistress, delivered letters." In Richard III he writes that the "King should not die before he (Clarence) be packed with post-horse up to heaven."

Even Hamlet castigates his mother's impetuosity by marking her "...wicked speed, to post with such dexterity to incestuous sheets." And Antonio in "The Tempest" declares that "She that from Naples can have no note, unless the sun were post, the man in the moon's too slow."

His frequent use of the image is evidence of its ubiquity – it must have been a common sight on English roads, just as in the Wild West the Pony Express was the main traffic of the day.

Horse-carried post was truly the e-mail of its time. Just as we slap a mouse-button, our Elizabethan forefathers slapped a scroll in a pannier hanging at the side of a snorting stallion, and he was off. These post-carriers covered anything from 70 to 180 miles in one day, depending on the weather and the road conditions. On March 25th 1603, the day following the Queen's death, Sir Robert Carey rode from London to Doncaster in a single day – 162 miles.

But all that, of course, was official business – a private individual like Shakespeare would have ridden between 20-30 miles a day, and stayed overnight in one of the hundreds of inns available en route. If wealthy enough he would have owned his own horse, or hired one at 12d for the first day, and 8d for each day thereafter. Each of the main carriers –

Greenaway included – would have had an office in one of the London Inns.

Were there carriages on the roads in 1596? Carts, of course, had been common for several centuries – two-wheeled, carrying agricultural produce or luggage. But in Shakespeare's lifetime the use of the carriage, or "caroches", was on the increase, so by the end of the 1590's wheeled traffic was outnumbering single horses, with carts and wagons taking the place of pack-horses with their loaded panniers.

This must have been a change in the visual landscape akin to the rise of the motor-car in the post-war years of the twentieth century: after-all, on the limestone-paved roads of cities, carriages must have effected the same increase of noise, and on the open highway and in small towns similar problems with traffic jams, congestion, and breakdowns. In fact, by 1601 a bill was put to Parliament to prevent congestion by carriages – it failed.

The poet John Taylor wrote of the appointment in 1564 of the Queen's Coachman, a Dutchman by the name of William Bonner. "A coach was a strange monster in those days," wrote Taylor, "and the sight of it put both horse and man into amazement."

At first coaches were just for the rich. That's not to say they were more comfortable than horseback – they weren't. Elizabeth herself complained to the French Ambassador in 1568 that "the aching pains she was suffering (were) in consequence of having been knocked about in a coach which had been driven a little too fast, only a few days before." About a century later the public vehicles were known as "hell-carts." They were four-wheeled, and although the insides were draped with cloth, they were utterly open at the sides, and what is more there were no springs – the body rested firmly on the axle. On the rutted and pot-holed roads of England any long journey would have been a juddering one - and in the absence of travel-sickness pills I think Shakespeare was far better off on a steed.

Yet carriages began to prove invaluable for the increase in demand for transportation in the Elizabethan age: John Dee sent his wife and family to Coventry on a coach from Mortlake in 1595; and Shakespeare himself makes reference to the growing popularity of wheeled traffic when he gets Mercutio to talk of carriages in the Queen Mab speech ("her wagon spokes made with long spinners' legs…")

So if this is indeed the place from where Shakespeare set off, let us dissolve the gate, see him enter the yard, greet his old pal Greenaway, give a coin to the boy who has carried his bags; let us see him greet his steed affectionately, a strong gelding who stamps and whinnies in his stalls. The playwright pats him with an affection that betrays a deep love for the animal.

For Shakespeare did indeed love horses.

In fact, it is not an exaggeration to say that he was obsessed with them.

54

CHAPTER FOUR

SHAKESPEARE'S HORSE

It is difficult now in our horseless age to understand just how significant and ubiquitous the horse was to our forefathers. In the pre-railway era everyone from beggar to King would have lived with horses, grown up with them, understood them, broken them, travelled with them, traded them, seen, heard and felt them every day of their lives on every street and lane in the country.

As a writer, Shakespeare loved horses - their iconography suffuses his plays. In "Antony & Cleopatra," for example, he mentions them no less than sixteen times. There is the well-known legend, of course, originating with Aubrey, of his first London job tying reins in the stable-yard of Burbage's Theatre off Shoreditch High Street. Is that where his love and knowledge of the animal began? Or was it the more obvious Stratford boyhood, in the fields and meadows of Warwickshire?

Stronger than legend are the first-hand accounts Shakespeare himself gives us of his equine life. In sonnet 50 he writes -

The beast that bears me, tired with my woe,

> *plods dully on, to bear that weight in me.*
> *The bloody spur cannot provoke him on,*
> *that sometimes anger thrusts into his hide,*
> *which heavily he answers with a groan,*
> *more sharp to me than spurring to his side;*
> *for that same groan doth put this in my mind;*
> *my grief lies onward, and my joy behind.*

Is this an account of one of the writer's leave-takings from his beloved London, of his long wearisome return home to the bosom of his provincial family in Stratford? If so, it must at times have been a long and boring journey. A weary horse, sagging lower beneath the gloomy playwright as his depression deepens. The cold road unwinding across the rainy heaths of Hounslow and Heathrow. He is trudging west to Uxbridge, through Beaconsfield, High Wycombe, Oxford, and eventually Stratford.

"...my grief lies onward, and my joy behind."

What was this "joy" that Shakespeare was leaving behind? The colourful, life-engaging world of the theatre - maybe a lover? And what was the "grief" that "(lay) onward?" His wife? *("there is no war and strife like a dark house and a detested wife.")*

There is no historical evidence proving the frequency of his journeys back to Stratford from his various homes in London: they are anecdotal, provided by John Aubrey in "Brief Lives." But Aubrey's anecdotage does rest on a sound base – the personal memories of Christopher Beeston, whose father worked with the playwright as an actor. Thus, the gossip tells us that Shakespeare made the journey roughly once a year at summertime, and preferred the route to Stratford through High Wycombe and Oxford. (To the modern mind, to visit your family only once a year smacks of estrangement. Perhaps this is so; but how different was

Shakespeare's life from that of the seaman, who might say farewell to his family for years on end?)

So, Shakespeare was obsessed with horses. Three quarters of the way through writing *Antony & Cleopatra,* Shakespeare came to Act IV scene XIV. He made Antony say to Eros:

> *Sometime we see a cloud that's dragonish,.*
> *A vapour sometime, like a bear, or lion,*
> *A tower'd citadel, a pendent rock,*
> *A forked mountain or blue promontory*
> *With trees upon it that nod unto the world,*
> *And mock our eys with air.*
> *Thou hast seen these signs,*
> *They are black vesper's pageants…*
> *That which is now a horse, even with a thought*
> *The rack dislimns, and makes it indistinct*
> *As water is in water.*

In those days clouds were signs, portents. Reading them was the soothsayer's art. But *dislimns?* The OED states that "dislimns" ie. effacing, the reverse of painting, is used by Shakespeare in this play only and does not occur in literature again until the nineteenth century.

The OED is not strictly correct. Ten years or so earlier, Shakespeare was writing "Venus and Adonis," published in 1593 as one of the poet's early attempts to outshine Marlowe, whose "Hero and Leander" appeared the year before. In a memorable passage consisting of what can only be described as a loving eulogy to horses, he writes:

> *But lo from forth a copse that neighbours by,*
> *A breeding jennet, lusty, young and proud,*
> *Adonis' trampling courser doth espy,*

58

And forth she rushes, snorts and neighs aloud…
Look when a painter would surpass the life
In limning out a well-proportioned steed,
His art with nature's workmanship at strife,
As if the dead the living should exceed.

"*Limning out a well-proportioned steed?*" Shakespeare is saying that the horse in the field is so solid and lifelike and resonant of what Huxley might have called the *"horseness"* of the horse, that it is like a painting. An artist attempts to outdo life. Like Coleridge's "painted ship upon a painted sea" Shakespeare can find no words to express the "thusness" of the beast except to say it aspires to the condition of art. Limning? – a painters technique of using light and shadow through paint to create the dimensions of life.

This remarkable echo of an image allows us a glimpse into the workings of the poet's mind. We are witnessing the birth of a thought. For such an unusual word - one which Shakespeare uses only twice in his entire canon - to be employed *both times* to illustrate the image of a horse, is beyond mere coincidence. The connection between horses and limning to us is tangential, beyond logic. So in realising that Shakespeare employs the word "dislimned" for Antony's horse in the clouds, we are hearing the poet remember his earlier use of the positive mode of it to describe the horse in "Venus & Adonis."

Yet it still begs the question – why "limning?" Why use the action of a painter to express, *twice* – and ten years or so apart – the image of a horse?

The only explanation is that painting techniques, and horses, were somehow connected in Shakespeare's mind.

But why?

59

In "Venus & Adonis" Shakespeare goes on to describe in minute detail the lusty young jennet.

Round-hoof'd, short-jointed, fetlocks shag and long,
Broad breast, full eye, small head, and nostril wide,
High crest, short ears, straight legs and passing strong,
Thin mane, thick tail, broad buttock, tender hide:
Look what a horse should have he did not lack,
Save a proud rider on so proud a back.

Dowden says "This passage of poetry has been admired; but is it poetry - or a paragraph from an advertisement of a horse sale?"

It may well be. Or, if not plagiarism of an advertisement, then perhaps a blow-by-blow description of an actual painted horse, hanging maybe on Shakespeare's wall not far from the desk where he was writing.

This realisation, if true – (and I cannot think of a better reason for the linking in Shakespeare's mind of the two images of painting and horses) - brought to sudden, jumping life the physical reality of Shakespeare himself. One can see the raised, varnished texture of the horse's portrait (the poet's own animal?) facing him as he worked; perhaps the creation of his painter/actor friend Richard Burbage, who is thought by scholars to have been responsible for the Chandos portrait.

Did Shakespeare own his own horse? I am advised by Eamonn Wilmott, one of this country's leading equine experts, that for a man of Shakespeare's wealth - and he was a millionaire - it would have been absolutely unthinkable that he did *not* own his own beast. Perhaps in "Venus & Adonis" he was describing his own horse in his own field. (But, being a work of the early 1590's, this was probably not the case).

60

If Shakespeare *did* own his own horse, as was probably the case, then maybe Greenaway looked after his fellow Stratfordian's animal, bringing it up to London as necessary, reuniting it with the playwright when his journey homeward beckoned. If so, it would have been an affectionate reunion that August morning in the yard of the Bell, the playwright patting the strong neck of his steed, a whinny of pleasure, a smile, a drink with his fellow traveller Greenaway before setting off on the long homeward journey…

CHAPTER FIVE

TO THE EDGE: NEWGATE TO
TYBURN

Whether on his own horse on another anonymous hired beast, Shakespeare, the gelding fully saddled up and his bags fastened to another pack-horse before him, would have plodded out of the yard of the Bell and turned left onto the cobbles or the dry August dust of Carter Lane.

The lane becomes Pilgrim Street as it bears right, winding round up the slope towards Ludgate Hill: it enters Ludgate extremely narrowly, the mouth being seemingly no wider than a doorway.

And the mouth of this narrow street is still there: in 2011 a rush of noise hits you as you leave the safe cool shadow of the lane. It must have been pretty much like this in 1596. Pilgrim Street comes out at exactly the spot where the old Ludgate used to stand: it was demolished in 1760. Directly opposite still stands the church of St. Martin's within Ludgate: Shakespeare would have seen it, but not this version – like so many, the church is Wren's.

I do not think Shakespeare came up Carter Lane this way – the traffic route is simply too narrow. I think he made his way back along Carter Lane towards St. Pauls, then up Ave Maria Street and Warwick Lane to Newgate Street. In fact, Stowe in his Survey of London gives a detailed explanation of why this is probably so: "Ludgate in the west was in this place so crossed and stopped up that the carriage through the city westward was forced to pass ... south down Ave Mary Lane, and again west through Bowyer Row to Ludgate: or else out of Cheap, or Watheling (Watling) Street, to turn south through old exchange; then west through Carter Lane, again north by Creed Lane, and then west to Ludgate: which passage, by reason of so often turning, was very cumbersome and dangerous both for horse and man: for remedy whereof a new gate was made, and so called (Newgate), by which men and cattle, with all manner of carriages, might pass more directly (as afore) from Aldgate, through West Cheap by Paul's, on the north side: through St. Nicholas Shambles and Newgate market, and from thence to any part westward over Oldbourne Bridge."

I think it highly likely, then, that Shakespeare would have followed his fellow-travellers not down the clogged-up bottleneck that would have been Carter Lane, but north up Creed Lane, a little further along from Addle Hill where the Bell Inn stood.

Had he been clip-clopping today through the cool shade of Creed Lane towards the furious highway of Ludgate Hill he would have passed several wine bars, a Prontaprint (an echo of the Elizabethan profession of the area) and a Costa Coffee on the corner. No time to pause for an espresso macchiato - the party crosses over Ludgate Hill, falling steeply to the left down towards the resplendent newly-built Gatehouse (completely rebuilt in 1586) in white stone, decorated on Shakespeare's side with the image of Queen Elizabeth, and on the outer side, by the figure of ancient King Lud.

Creed Lane, north of Carter Lane, along which Shakespeare trotted on the beginning of his journey out of London. Photo: Basher Eyre 2008.

Gustave Doré's "Ludgate Hill - A block in the Street" -- from London, A Pilgrimage, 1872. In crossing Ludgate Hill in the 1590's Shakespeare may have found it only slightly less congested than Dore's depiction.

... and Ludgate Hill today. Photo: The Lud 2006.

Over crowded Ludgate Hill then to Ave Maria Lane, which is almost a direct crossing; now boasting a Sportsworld, a Vidal Sassoon, an M & S Simply Food on its corner. Further up on ether side, more 1980's humanless geometry passing for architecture; but then, suddenly, on the left, we have Amen Corner, a sacred island of history amidst the pale modern blocks – and this Shakespeare would have passed: a wise old courtyard, a warm pocket of 17th century buildings fronted by crooked black lamps. Offices of the Cathedral, they may be slightly later structures than the ones the playwright passed, and now the inner courtyard has a child's playground, which may not have been there in 1596.

A solitary tyre hangs motionless on a rope. No one comes and goes in the darkening square. All the houses and offices of Amen Corner seem empty. As it is a Sunday are they all in nearby St. Pauls, going about their duties?

Adorning the front entrance gateway of the courtyard are numerous plaques: awards from the Worshipful Company of Gardeners.

Ave Maria Lane. Photo: Danny Robinson 2007.

Ave Maria Lane becomes without announcement Warwick Lane - more 1980's brutalism in Warwick Square - but then another sudden smile from the sixteenth and seventeenth centuries with an old redbrick cry of greeting from the Cutler's Hall: a splendid golden elephant hanging above the entrance – though precisely why the noble cutlery-makers should have chosen a pachyderm as the symbol of their trade is beyond me: perhaps it was the result of a drunken evening spent trying to come up with a brand-logo. "I know," suggests one particularly inebriated Master Cutler, as he leans forward clutching his tankard, "an elephant!" And they all cheer.

So there it is, a shining-gold trunked beacon in what is now a dull grey street of offices. It appears that the Cutlers weren't always here, however – they ousted the Royal College of Physicians from the building in 1825, after the doctors had resided there since 1674.

Across the top of Cutler's Hall: "Pour parvenir au bonne foy." I don't know what it means. "For the love of forks?"

The Great Fire swept away the Warwick Lane of Shakespeare's time, but Chambers Book of Days in 1832 records its pre-fire state: "Few of the thoroughfares of old London have undergone such mutations of fortune as may be traced in Warwick-lane...once the site of the house of the famed Beauchamps, Earls of Warwick, afterwards distinguished by including in its precincts the College of Physicians, now solely remarkable for an abundance of those private shambles which are still permitted to disgrace the English metropolis. In the coroners' rolls of five centuries ago, we read of mortal accidents which befell youths in attempting to steal apples in the neighbouring orchards of Paternoster-row and Ivy-lane, then periodically redolent of fruit-blossoms. The College of Physicians, built by Wren to replace a previous fabric burnt down in the Great Fire, may still be seen on the west side of the lane, but sunk into the condition of a butcher's shop. Here the physicians met until the year 1825, when they removed to their newly-built College in Pall Mall East. The interior of the edifice in Warwick-lane was convenient and sumptuous; and one of the minute accounts tells us that in the garrets were dried the herbs for the use of the Dispensary."

Chambers continues: "In the lane are two old galleried inns, which carry us back to the broad-wheeled travelling wagons of our forefathers. About midway, on the east side, is the Bell Inn. Before the Great Fire a market was kept in Newgate-street, where there was a market-house formed, and a middle row of sheds, which afterwards were converted into houses, and inhabited by butchers, tripe-sellers, &c. The stalls in the open street grew dangerous, and were accordingly removed into the open space between Newgate-street and Paternoster-row, formerly the orchards already mentioned: and here were the houses of the Prebends of St Paul's, overgrown with ivy: whence ivy-lane takes its name, although amidst the turmoil of the market, with the massive dome of St Paul's on one side, and that of the old College of Physicians on the other, it is hard to associate the place with the domain of a nymph so lovely as Pomona."

The other galleried inn of Warwick-lane was the Oxford Arms, within a recess on the west side, nearly adjoining the houses of St Paul's in Amen-corner. Until its demolition it was, according to Chambers, one of the best specimens of the old London inns remaining in the metropolis - "... the inn-yard... has, on three of its sides, two stories of balustraded wooden galleries, with exterior staircases leading to the chambers on each floor: the fourth side being occupied by stabling, built against part of old London wall. The house was an inn with the sign of the Oxford Arms before the Great Fire, as appears by the following advertisement in the London Gazette for March, 1672-3, No. 762:

> *These are to give notice, that Edward Bartlett, Oxford carrier, hath removed his inn, in London, from the Swan, at Holborn-bridge, to the Oxford Arms, in Warwick-lane, where he did inn before the Fire: his coaches and wagons going forth on their usual days,—Mondays, Wednesdays, and Fridays. He hath also a*

> *hearse, with all things convenient, to carry a corpse to any part of England.*

As Shakespeare reached the top of Warwick Lane, then, in order to turn left into Newgate Street, he would have circumnavigated the numerous meat-stalls above-described, the rather more noble sight of Greyfriar's monastery then meeting the playwright's eyes. Dissolved in 1538 like many of the religious orders across the capital it would then have been Christ's Hospital, built in 1552 and demolished in 1962. What is striking is the number of large hospitals that existed across Elizabethan London – a few yards up the road they had St. Bartholemews, he'd already passed St. Bethlehem's. Shakespeare's London appears to have been dominated by three types of building: the church, pandering to the spirit; the hospital, pandering to the body; and the Guild buildings and shops, pandering mainly to the stomach. 'Twas ever thus, I suppose – man's hierarchy of needs.

★

Greyfriars, in its new incarnation as Christ's Hospital, performed perhaps a nobler function than its original one as a home for friars: that of looking after orphans. Stow: "In the year 1552 began the repairing of the Grey Friar's House for the poor fatherless children; and in the month of November the children were taken into the same, to the number of almost four hundred. On Christmas Day in the afternoon, while the Lord Mayor and aldermen rode to St. Paul's, the children of Christ's Hospital stood, from St. Lawrence Lane end in Cheap, towards Paul's, all in one livery of russet cotton, three hundred and forty in number; and in Easter next they were in blue at the Spital, and so have continued ever since.

Looking back down Warwick Lane from Newgate Street, EC4, including a view of Cutler's Hall on the right. Photo: John Salmon 2009.

What a magnificent sight this row of rescued children would have been, a living testimony to the magnanimity of the age. One of them in earlier times was George Peele, fellow playwright and friend of Shakespeare, who grew up here as an orphan.

Within the friary itself were literally hundreds of defaced monuments. The iconoclasm of the new Protestant era is something difficult to comprehend today, and its effect upon the sensibility of the intelligentsia like Shakespeare must have been profound. The broad populace, I believe, would have swum with the tide and enjoyed the tearing down of the monuments as a basic satisfaction of the herd instinct. Commentators state that Shakespeare's reluctance to make an open statement of "what he believed in" do not always, I think, take into account the extraordinary risk that anyone would have faced in so doing. We've already seen how the simple cross at Cheapside was vandalised on numerous occasions across the years simply for displaying the image of Mary, and even the baby Jesus. Shakespeare's father himself, as Bailiff of Stratford, was charged with whitewashing over the sacred images in the Guild Chapel in Stratford, pictures the young Shakespeare never saw as a grammar school boy because the defacement took place four years he was born. This was an age akin to Stalinism, to Chinese Communism tearing down the statues of Buddha in Tibet, airbrushing entire generations of Catholic aristocrats out of history – dynasties of rulers that Shakespeare himself may have felt a certain tug of love for. Was he a Catholic? The debate continues, but I feel certain that he would not have agreed one iota with the value of defacing a statue or smashing a piece of sculpture. I feel that he would have felt that to be an act of spiritual death, of pointless herdism.

As he turned into Newgate Street Shakespeare would have seen, on his right, the churchyard of St. Botolph's further up St. Martins-le-Grand. Overarched by twisting sycamores, its black iron gates enclose today a neat patch of lawn, with wooden benches for lunching office workers and tombstones long since cleared away and stacked up against the church wall like piles of unwanted volumes in a bookshop. In its yard is an arcade, the brainchild of the sentimental Victorian painter G. F. Watts - a simple wooden loggia housing a series of art-nouveau ceramic tiles, decoratively cracked, each one telling the spellbinding tale of a tragic, heartstirring death. *"Solomon Galaman, aged 11. Died of injuries September 6th 1901, after saving his little brother from being run over in Commercial St. 'Mother I saved him, but I could not save myself!'"* Each tile a faded

Christchurch Greyfriars, Newgate Street. Photo: John Salmon 2009.

sepia photograph in ceramic form, a sort of Victorian "999," a dramatic snapshot of a Dickensian London long since gone, conjuring up the city's danger, smell and colourful violence. *"Thomas Griffin, Fitter's Labourer, who on April 12th 1899, in a boiler explosion in Battersea sugar refinery, was fatally scalded in returning to search for his mate."* You can almost see the rivers of burning sugar, smell the air heavy and sweet with flame, glimpse Thomas Griffin's frantic battle against the sulphurous swell of flavoured fire. *"Elizabeth Boxall, aged 17, of Bethnal Green, who died of injuries received in trying to save a child from a runaway horse. June 20th 1888."* So down through Newgate Market. The Agas map of the 1560's shows the trellis tables and stalls in the middle of the street, laden with chops, joints.

Much of Newgate Street now is bulky steel and glass; a massive characterless Axa building on the left hand side, but an old, grand but slightly shabby-genteel eighteenth century parade on the right, just past where the orphans of Christ's Hospital would have stood: *Leonard Jay's shoe store*, *William Hayford's florists* – retail establishments now oddly out of place in the acreage of space given over to mere wage slavery and not the purchase of shoes or flowers. They remain as an echo of what the street once was before the 1980's: normal, inhabited, strolled down by local citizens. Local citizens now there are none.

So smash down the Axa building and go back in time four hundred years and here was Newgate Market – flower-sellers on the south side and the meat stalls on the north, being near to Smithfield. St. Nicholas Shambles at the west end of Newgate Street was the home of butchers. No slaughtering took place here – it was forbidden within the gates of the City in 1516 – so the animals were apparently killed in the vicinity of Knightsbridge and the carcasses transported to Newgate. The smell as Shakespeare passed down the street on 1st August 1596 would have been a fragrant intermingling of flesh and bloom, pork and poppy, beef and begonia. Maybe the faint whiff of corn and meal from behind him as Newgate Street blended into West Cheap.

Newgate itself was demolished in 1777: as Shakespeare passed through he may have heard the clank of chains, the odd cry of an inmate, seen the huge doors swing open roughly and a four-horse carriage gallop out bearing a rack or a cart behind carrying a condemned man the mile through Holborn, St. Giles High Street, Tyburn Lane (the present Oxford Street), to the gallows at today's Marble Arch. If it was execution day, crowds would be lining the streets already: tales are told of cocksure prisoners yelling jokes to the onlookers outside taverns – "I'll buy you a pint on the way back!" – jocularity in the face of death the hallmark of an age of plague, disease and a life that was for most, nasty, brutish and short.

Just outside the gate itself he would have seen on his left the broad courtyard housing the Old Bailey. New and expansive now in its eighteenth-century stone, the older Old Bailey would have been a grimmer, more forbidding place. On his right after the gate was Gilford Street, now Giltspur Street, leading to Smithfield, or "Smooth Field," – a wide expanse of meadows whereon the youth of London would sport in mock-jousting, and horse and cattle-dealers would gather; developing over the decades into the meat-dealing centre of the capital.

Had he glanced right, then, as he passed Giltspur Street, Shakespeare would have seen St. Bartholemew's Hospital on its eastern side. Opposite the hospital stood the Fortune of War Inn – an office block now but still containing, set in its outer wall, a statue of the "Golden Boy of Pie Corner," commemorating the Great Fire of 1666. Being conveniently situated opposite St. Bart's Hospital, the Fortune of War became a habitual clandestine meeting-place of body-snatchers. Spiriting their catches at the dead of night, having bought them from Tyburn or fished them out of the Thames or purchased them freshly dead from an unscrupulous gaoler at nearby Newgate Prison, they would carry them to an upstairs room in the tavern and wait for the surgeons to dash across from St. Barts with their coins. It is said that on occasions a surgeon would be taken upstairs to this secret room and be greeted by dozens of corpses, all sitting round the edge of the room looking for all the world like normal everyday punters, apart from the fact that they weren't quaffing ale.

For us, now, crossing Holborn Viaduct does not seem particularly dramatic, but to an Elizabethan there must have been a huge sense of escape, a feeling that you were actually leaving London. To us the street simply becomes Holborn, the edge of London a further eight miles away in Acton or even Southall. But for Shakespeare there was no such thing as a suburb; once you passed through one of the great gates, that was it, you were not in London any more. St. Giles-in-the-fields was precisely that – a village in the fields.

Our sense of towns and cities sprawling into suburbs and melting into one another is peculiarly modern: to reconstruct the landscape of Elizabethan England one must realise that most towns were small and all cities surrounded by gated walls. The population of London was approximately 200,000, and Norwich, the largest provincial town in the country, could be described as "either a City in an orchard, or an orchard in a city, so equally are houses and trees blended in it."

So whilst not quite considering himself in the country after passing through Newgate, Shakespeare would certainly feel as though he were not in a city anymore. Outside the gate there were grand houses, to be sure – the great Inns of Court lining Holborn and humbler shops, but there were also orchards, fields and large gardens – the Inns of Court were, after all, Lincoln's Inn *Fields,* Grays Inn *Fields.*

Just outside the gate Shakespeare would have seen, on his right, the church of St. Sepulchre-without-Newgate. Its beautiful tower is still intact, the walls, tower and porch having survived the Great Fire and re-worked by Wren's masons. Its mullioned windows would have sparkled in the sunlight below the fleur-de-lis inlets. Now, as then, its rain-smoothed bone-white spire would have been fanned by the wings of resting seagulls, overlooking Snow Hill.

For us, Newgate Street forges ahead to cross Farringdon Street on the Holborn Viaduct, but for Shakespeare the highway would have continued as Snow Hill, which led down the slopes of the riverbank to the bridge of Old Bourne ('Hol-born.'

On the right just a few yards down Snow Hill stood the Saracen's Head, demolished in 1868. Now, at the bottom of Snow Hill, can be made out the crumbling neglected bulk of Smithfield Market. Shamefully abandoned and allowed to rot, the old market is dying. Ferns and budlia sprout from loosened masonry in its crevices; inside, dead ferns press and curl against the dusty panes. A dark archway is barred with a black rusty zigzag grille: inside, empty gutted meat-stalls held up by decaying green pillars murmur with flies and the ghosts of a hundred butchers.

An air of doom hangs over West Smithfield today. Faded names stare mournfully from forgotten boarded-up shops – *Terence Knight wholesale Meat; Village Pork.* Plans have been drawn up for a new, giant, glass thing that will straddle the area like a transparent flimsy colossus. It all looks remarkably impossible, garish, clean and boring, and will kill off the old Smithfield forever.

St. Sepulchre-without-Newgate.
Photo: Tony Hisgate 2010.

Junction of Snow Hill and Smithfield Street. Photo: Basher Eyre 2008.

The old open air Smithfield Market in 1855. Illustrated London News 1855. In Shakespeare's day it would have been open fields used for military training and horse fairs.

Yet this is the place Shakespeare would have crossed the river; the view to his right would have been of broad green fields, crowded yes with a horse-fair and a cattle-market, but green nevertheless. Looking left as he crossed the Old Bourne Bridge, the River Fleet would have flowed down to the Thames towards Blackfriar's Stairs – no bridge yet. The Thames' crowded wharves, wrote Camden, "shaded with masts and sails," gave it the appearance of "a wooded grove." And along its banks, stretching from Temple Stairs to King's Bridge, grand palaces and riverside houses, each with its garden and water-gate.

Holborn Viaduct today. Shakespeare would have crossed the river on an old wooden bridge. Photo: Basher Eyre, 2008.

Up on the viaduct on the left is now Gresham House complete with statue of Thomas Gresham, the present bridge of red ironwork, winged lions, figures of justice and temperance. And over the bridge, the site of the former Mayor's house, Henry Fitz-Elyer, 1189-1212. Then the City Temple United Reformed Church, rebuilt after being bombed in the Second World War, hiding a narrow Plum-tree Court, just visible now from the road. Did Shakespeare pass a beautiful orchard of plum trees here, as he walked his horse up the hill past St. Andrew's? The slope down to the old Fleet River is still steep here – both churches are now well below street-level, which of course they weren't for Shakespeare.

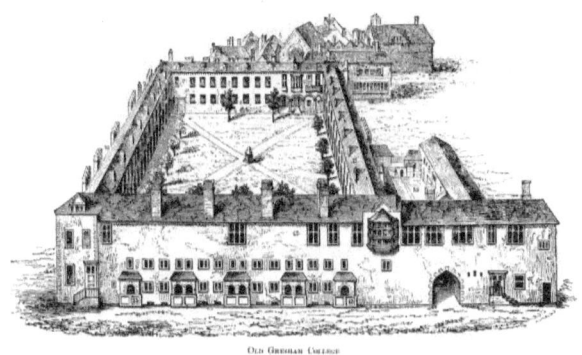

Gresham College as Shakespeare would have passed it, on his left at the beginning of High Holborn. Record of the Royal Society (1912); Unknown artist, after an illustration in John Ward, Lives of the Professors of Gresham College (1740)

Holborn Circus now, with Prince Albert on horseback, forever lifting his hat to a gigantic Sainsbury's Support Centre opposite. The building is completely transparent. Are British architects currently obsessed with transparency? Does an architecture degree these days include a module on voyeurism? I imagine an office argument taking place, in perfect visibility of the passers-by in the street below. And what's more, why do people who shop at Sainsbury's need a support centre? For psychological damage, perhaps.

On the right, the huge red gothic Prudential Building. They currently have my money, and won't give it back until I'm sixty-five. I need it now, but they won't give it to me. I contemplate entering the building and creating a fuss about it, but instead I have a pastrami sandwich in a Starbucks.

As now, Shakespeare's Holborn was a broad highway, the chief features of which were the huge Inns of Court, essentially colleges for trainee lawyers. The legal industry was becoming vast in Elizabethan England, each inn specialising in different aspects of the law. A middle-class intelligentsia was being generated in these centres of learning, and it is precisely this class of young gentleman who formed the bulk of the audience at the Blackfriar's Theatre, for which Shakespeare wrote his masterpieces Macbeth, King Lear, Antony and Cleopatra, and Coriolanus.

So, Staple Inn, Barnard's Inn, Gray's Inn, Lincoln's Inn... in Gray's inn in the early 1590's the law students were privy to seeing Shakespeare's early play, "Comedy of Errors" performed in the great hall. And between Staple Inn and Chancery Lane Gerard the Herbalist had a house, growing tobacco in his gardens, and "love-apples," - tomatoes.

The famous long frontage of Staple Inn is one of the only remaining Elizabethan buildings in London, now housing a

Vodafone Store, Lipman and Sons suits, and Sherington's Cigars, Snuff and Gifts. The building is almost exactly as Shakespeare would have trotted past it in 1596, apart from the fact that it would not have been black and white but pale ochre.

Staple Inn much as Shakespeare would have seen it, on his left as he passed along High Holborn. Illustrated London News 1886.

... and the same buildings today. Photo: Edward, 2005.

In 1541 an Act of Parliament was passed, ordering the "western road of London, from Holborne Bars to St. Giles-in-the-Fields, to be paved, as far as there was any habitation of both sides of the street." So Shakespeare would have ridden on paved road until he reached the village of St. Giles, in what is now Bloomsbury.

Gazing northwards across the fields the honeyed stone of Southampton House glows through the summer oaks. Now Bloomsbury Square, the house seven years later was the venue of a special performance of "Love's Labour's Lost," for Queen Anne; starring Burbage and probably Shakespeare himself in the role of Thomas Berowne. Southampton played a huge role in the poet's life, as patron and friend, and perhaps fellow idealist – Southampton's father had been a Catholic just as Shakespeare's father had been, both having been involved in the Campion conspiracy. This bond of faith between their parents may have eased the creative bond between the two men which so plainly existed.

In a map of Westminster, by Norden, dated 1593, no houses are shown eastward of Drury Lane; but building must have commenced very shortly after this, for in Speed's Map of Westminster, in his "Great Britain," the beginning of Great Queen Street is indicated, together with a continuation of the houses on both sides of Drury Lane. The chief part of the village of St. Giles in the sixteenth century was composed of houses standing on the north of the highway which led westward from Holborn to Tyburn, and whose gardens stretched behind them to St. Blemund's Dyke – the orgin of "Bloomsbury."

In Ralph Agas' map it figures as a small village, or rather a small group of cottages, with their respective garden-plots nestling around the walls of the hospital – the first St. Giles Church was the centre of a large leper hospital. The

Hospital of St. Giles-in-the-Fields stood within a large walled compound delineated by today's Charing Cross Road, Shaftesbury Avenue and St. Giles High Street. The chapel of this Hospital served both the leper inmates and the population of the village of St. Giles, which grew around a new monastic foundation. It is possible that the hospital was placed at the western end of what later called "the old village" (Alde Wych), situated where High Holborn and Drury Lane now meet.

Over three hundred years after Shakepeare passed Drury Lane on his left, a performance of his play King John takes place at the Drury Lane Theatre in 1865.
The Illustrated London News, Dec. 9, 1865, p. 556

The Hospital was dissolved in 1539, and in 1545 Henry V111 bestowed it and its precincts, but not its chapel, on John Dudley. Dudley was executed in 1553; after the accession of Elizabeth, his surviving son Robert Dudley, who became the Earl of Leicester in 1564, appears to have received back the manor-house of St. Giles, which lay to the north-west of the Church and fronted Hog Lane (later Charing Cross Road), and it became known as Dudley House. Here lived for many years until her death aged 90 in 1669 Alicia Lady Dudley, his wife. Robert Dudley deserted her in 1605, when he went to live in Italy with a mistress.

St. Giles in the Fields, Bloomsbury. Photo: Mike Quinn 2009.

So Shakespeare would have ridden past Dudley House on his right, in August 1596, past the long Blemund's ditch with its various footbridges. Was Alicia Dudley in her garden as he passed, enjoying happier times nine years before her husband abandoned her? A moment before, he would have ridden past the ancient stone cross of St. Giles, which seems to have stood near what is now the north end of Endell Street.

St. Giles had an historical resonance for Shakespeare: it was here in 1413 that the Lollards gathered, in the fields adjoining St. Giles's Hospital, headed by Sir John Oldcastle

– the historical proto-type for Falstaff - who afterwards was executed on the spot, being hung in chains over a slow fire.

St. Giles Pound – situated approximately where Shaftesbury Avenue bisects High Holborn, was the principal place of execution outside the city before Tyburn took over. Ballard and four others who were concerned in Babington's Plot in 1586 were executed at St. Giles Pound. The unusual width of High Holborn west of the junction with Drury Lane enabled it in days gone by to serve as a kind of village green, under the name Broad St Giles's.

There was no Charing Cross Road in the sixteenth century leading from St. Giles down to St. James and Westminster - there were no continuous rows of houses in that south-west direction. At the point where Tottenham Court Road now intersects Oxford Street, there was a notice, at the top of a narrow lane running across where is now Soho, saying *"The Road to Reading."* It led, bending, no further than the top of the Haymarket, where the traffic then proceeded West along Piccadilly all the way to Reading and Bath. There was another narrow lane parallel to it, Hedge Lane, leading past the corner of Leicester Fields, becoming in centuries to come, Leicester Square. The first era of building began a little before 1600, so Shakespeare could have been passing a few building sites as he rode. By around 1600 Holborn and St. Giles's were nearly connected together. After the wall of the hospital was pulled down, houses began to be built on the east, west, and south sides of the church, and on both sides of St. Giles's Street new dwellings multiplied. Ten years later saw the commencement of Great Queen Street, and a continuation of the houses down both sides of Drury Lane. By 1623 897 houses were rated. So Shakespeare's annual or bi-annual journey witnessed the early piecemeal beginnings of the West End. He passed St. Giles Church on his left, Lady

Alicia Dudley's manor house on his right, and the sign saying *"Road to Reading,"* pointing towards what is now Shaftesbury Avenue.

And so to Oxford Street. Variously called Uxbridge Road and Tyburn Road, the great highway west follows the line of the Via Trinobantina, one of the military roads of the Romans, which bounded the north side of what is now Hyde Park, and continued thence to Old Street (Eald Street).

In Ralph Agas's map of 1560 the space to the north of Oxford Street , then "the way to Uxbridge," was open country, with fields and hedges, and dotted irregularly with trees; and in Vertue's plan, about a century later, the only building seen between the village of St. Giles and Primrose Hill is the little solitary church of Marlebone - and still further away in the fields the little church of St. Pancras, "all alone, old, and weather-beaten." Pennant tells us how that "the Lord Mayor and his brethren of the City used to repair to a building called the City Banqueting House, on the north side of Oxford Street near Tyburn Brook on horseback, attended by their ladies in waggons, to inspect the conduits, and then to partake of their banquet."

John Timbs writes in his "Curiosities of London:"—"In a map of 1707, on the south side, King Street, near Golden Square, is perfect to Oxford Road, between which and Berwick Street are fields; thence to St. Giles's is covered with buildings, but westward not a house is to be seen; the northern side of Oxford Road contains a few scattered buildings, but no semblance of streets westward of Tottenham Court Road." This would appear to have been literally the case, for a plan of 1708, which he also mentions, shows the "Adam and Eve" as "a detached road-side public-house." It stood, according to this plan, in the "Dung-field," near the present Adam and Eve Court, almost opposite Poland Street; in an adjoining field is represented "the boarded house of Figg, the prize-fighter," standing quite isolated from other buildings.

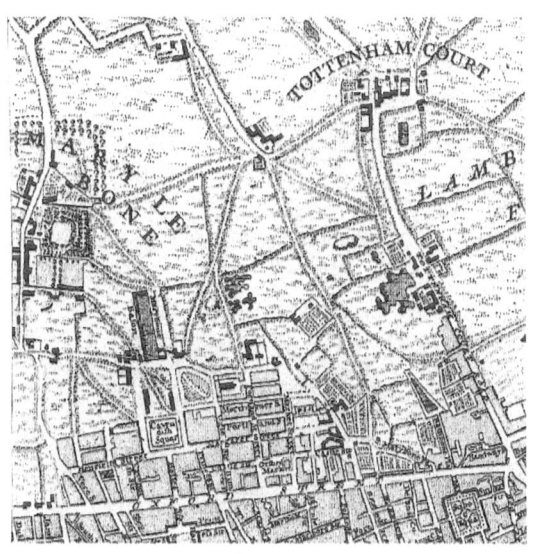

John Rocque's map of Marylebone & Tottenham Court, 1741. When Shakespeare rode along Oxford Street in the 1590's, scarcely any of the streets radiating off the main highway would have existed, merely as a few lanes leading to farms.

So a century earlier, the whole stretch of highway west of Holborn must have been even more desolate and rural. Indeed, the only buildings Shakespeare probably passed on his way to Tyburn would have been the Adam and Eve Inn, Figg's house or its predecessor, St. Marylebone Church peeping through the trees on his right, an inn called the

"Rose of Normandy," maybe Marylebone Manor House, and the odd cottage.

That the street in its early days must have been anything but a pleasant or safe thoroughfare for travellers is pretty clear from Pennant's remark that he remembered it "a deep hollow road, and full of sloughs, with here and there a ragged house, the lurking-place of cut-throats; insomuch," he adds, "that I never was taken that way by night in my hackney-coach to a worthy uncle's, who gave me lodgings in his house in George Street, but I went in dread the whole way."

The name Marylebone is said to be a corruption or an abridgement of "St. Mary-le-Bourne on the Brook," so called from a small chapel dedicated to the Blessed Virgin which stood on the banks of a small brook, or bourne, or burn, which still runs down from the slopes of Hampstead, passing under Allsop Buildings, where, of course, it is arched over. This is the derivation of the name as given by most writers, who compare with it the termination of Ty*burn*. Some writers have asserted that the parish was itself originally called Tybourne, or Tyburn, from the brook (bourne), a name which gradually was exchanged for Marylebourne or Marylebone. But whatever may be its derivation, four centuries ago it was still a rural spot, and Macaulay reminds us that even at the end of the reign of Charles II "cattle fed and sportsmen wandered with dogs and guns over the site of the borough of Marylebone." It was, in fact, nothing more than a small country village, separated from London by green fields.

In a map published in 1742 we see the small village church of Marylebone standing quite alone in the fields. It is approached by two narrow zigzag lanes, one winding up from about the bottom of the east side of Stratford Place - then the western boundary of all continuous houses-following the line of what is still called Marylebone Lane; the other lane crosses the fields diagonally from Tottenham Court Road. This lane, the northern end of which is now called Marylebone High Street, was in olden times a footway through the fields from Brook Field, the site of which is now covered by Brook Street, to Marylebone Manor House. It was an old rural lane, along which the farm-horses went to the great city to market from the farmers of the outlying districts.

The "Rose of Normandy," a public-house in Marylebone High Street, is probably the oldest house in the parish. It is described in the *Gentleman's Magazine*, vol. lxxxiii., p. 524, as having had, in the year before the Restoration, "outside a square brick wall, set with fruit-trees, gravel walks 204 paces long, 7 broad; the circular wall 485 paces long, 6 broad; the centre square a bowling-green, 112 paces one way, 88 another; all, except the first, double set with quickset hedges, full-grown, and kept in excellent order, and indented like town walls." Maybe Shakespeare glimpsed the Rose of Normandy as he passed, or the Manor – he certainly would have seen the old church of St. Marylebone, which had been built before the Reformation, but pulled down in 1741.

Smith's "Book for a Rainy Day" published in the eighteenth century, tells us just how rural the area north of Oxford Street was even a century and a half after Shakespeare's journey. "The houses of the north end of Newman Street," at the time Mr. Smith was a lad, "... commanded a view of the fields, over hillocks of ground... of the distant heights of Highgate, Hampstead, Primrose Hill, and Harrow. The south and east ends of Queen Anne and Marylebone Streets were then unbuilt: the space consisted of fields to the west corner of Tottenham Court Road, thence to the extreme end of High Street,

Marylebone Gardens, Marylebone Basin, and another pond then called "Cockney Ladle," which were the terror of many a mother.

He'd been riding for a mere half hour or so but already Shakespeare was crossing open country. If not quite wilderness, the western reaches of Oxford Street were as untamed then as Salisbury Plain today. His route was clear, well-trodden, and long-established. Harrison outlines Shakespeare's trip between London and Oxford thus, albeit in reverse: *"Whatelie, Thetisford, Stocking-church, East Wickham, Beaconsfield, Uxbridge."* And Mr. Haliwell-Phillips in his "Life of Shakespeare" lays out an account of some Stratford people who travelled from their home town to London on business for the Corporation in 1592:

Charges laid out when we went to Court:
Paid for our horsemeat the firs night at Oxford... 2s 8d
And for our own charges the same night... 2s 2d
The second night at Islip for our supper..... 2s 4d
The third day for our bait and our horses
At Hook Norton... 12d
And for walking our horses at Tetsworth and
elsewhere.... 3d
Sum for this journey... 12s 1d

Any picturesqueness he may have experienced as he passed Marylebone Church and the Banqueting House, set back from the roadside in flower-strewn fields, would have faded from his mind as he approached a bridge which crossed a narrow sparkling brook flowing north to south. For here was the smell of death, of blood in the dirt. He was approaching the killing fields of Tyburn.

CHAPTER SIX

THE KILLING FIELDS: TYBURN TO
SHEPHERD'S BUSH

In passing over the Tyburn River at the top of the Western end of what is now Oxford Street - crossing a stone bridge at the bottom of what is now Edgware Road, with a conduit nearby - Shakespeare was entering a grim arena of state brutality. Here was murder as pageantry, scapegoatery, religious massacre, racial bigotry (the crowd laughed openly at the Jewish Lopez as he mounted the scaffold in 1594) and social control. Here was death as theatrical spectacle, a culling staged to terrify, delight and subdue the masses. In the fearful police state that was sixteenth century London the junction of Tyburn Lane, Uxbridge Rd. and the road north, now Edgware Road, was for several hundred years the principal locale of government blood-letting right up until the nineteenth century, when public executions ceased and hangings retreated behind the walls of Newgate.

That Shakespeare attended public executions and witnessed the blood-lust of the London mob as the cart drew close to the scaffold of Tyburn is highly likely: his work bristles with execution imagery. Mob scenes also feature heavily in the plays, from the history epics to Julius Caesar, where the mob even tears a poet to pieces, and the unperformed *"Thomas More."*

Illustration, said to be from about 1680, of the permanent gallows at Tyburn, which stood where Marble Arch now stands. This necessitated a three-mile cart ride in public from Newgate prison to the gallows. Huge crowds collected on the way and followed the accused to Tyburn. They were used as the gallows for London offenders from the 16th century until 1759. National Archives.

Strangely, his attitude to mobs is one of the few authorial consistencies one can point to in the plays - his judgement is uniformly one of distaste. Crowds of humanity in Shakespeare are rabble - he dehumanises them; they are palpably not a collection of individuals but a monstrous collective thing-in-itself, capable of acts of madness fuelled by the worst resources and desires of the human brain – revolution, destruction, the death-instinct.

In Shakespeare's day the Tyburn river had two arms, one crossing Oxford Street and travelling down to what is still called Brook Street, the other further West following the line of Westbourne Terrace down to the Serpentine. As he crossed this second bridge over into what is now Bayswater Road, Shakespeare would have been shaded by rows of elm trees that grew tall along its banks. It was from these elms that the first victims of executions were hung, until the executions were moved to the area of Marble Arch, and the gallows was moved there from St. Giles Pound. Brook Mews and Elms Mews still hold the memory of this gushing stream. Tyburn was chosen after complaints from the parishioners of St. Sepulchre-without-Newgate, concerned by the burial of convicted felons alongside their loved ones. A letter written by Fleetwood to Lord Burghley states that they would "not suffer a traytor's corpses to be layed in the earth where their parents, wyeffs, children, kynred, maisters, and old neighbours did rest: and so his carcas was returned to the burial ground near to Tyborne."

It was in Tyburn then that Shakespeare probably witnessed in 1594 the hanging of Lopez, the Jewish advisor to Elizabeth who, in the conspiratorial melting-pot which was Elizabethan government, fell prey to the gossip, rumour and accusation endemic to her rule. In the foul and rank atmosphere of favour-currying, friendships fell on the sword of treachery, and scapegoats were made of those who grew too close to the unmarried monarch. The historian William Camden, who was also at the death, wrote that Lopez roused himself to a dignity on the scaffold, declaring that he "loved the Queen as well as he loved Jesus Christ. Which," Camden continues, "moved no small laughter in the standers-by."

Did Shakespeare witness this horrifying laughter? If he did, he may have commemorated his reaction to it by writing, several years later, his famous demolition of a racial stereotype in Shylock. He may also have attended the execution of the Earl of Essex in 1601, and would then have seen the celebrated Derrick, the Jacobean Albert Pierrepoint, who leant his name to the crane for hoisting cargo on and off ships.

Beyond the area of the scaffold lay more open country on either side – both north and south of what is now the Bayswater Road was undeveloped. "A Great Plan of the Great Road from Tybourne to Uxbridge," surveyed by Leddiard in 1769, shows huge gravel pits on either side of the highway, presumably for the making of bricks and mortar; the pits on the right hand side of the road stretching as far as what is today Kensal New Town. A lane forked north to Paddington, still there - a one-way system now taking traffic up to the A40 – in 1596 a brick bridge over the Westbourne which, having travelled from South Hampstead, divides Paddington from Bayswater and feeds the Serpentine. On the right hand side of the road Shakespeare would have seen the conduit dubbed "Baynard's Watering Place," later contracted to "Bayswater."

A cluster of houses at Notting Hill shown on John Rocque's map of 1745 is so small it hardly merits the description of a village, so when Shakespeare passed through there must have been even less signs of habitation. The landscape was manorial estate but still wild country. A boatman on the Thames in 1596, looking north, would have seen fields and meadows, the spire of Kensington Church, and nothing but wooded hills all the way to the horizon. Half a mile on, if Shakespeare had gazed north he would have seen Notting Barns Manor - "Notten Barns" - which by 1745 had given the area the name of "Notting Hill." Formerly Abbey lands reverting to state ownership with the Dissolution, the manor was occupied at the time of Shakespeare's journey by William Cecil, Lord Burghley.

Huge orchards of nut trees festooned the slopes surrounding the area that was rural right up to the nineteenth century, when the Ladbroke estate was formed, parcelling the acreage then into neat regency avenues, crescents and squares. When the estate was being built a stone coffin was excavated containing the skeleton of a Roman, proving that this was indeed the road to Silchester – for Romans did not bury their dead within city walls but along the side of a highway.

Had he glanced south as he travelled home eight or nine years later, in 1605, Shakespeare would have seen builders busy at work on Holland House, a mansion being built for Sir Walter Cope, property dealer, moneylender and merchant and friend of James I. It would have been the only grand building he passed on this stretch of the road to Uxbridge – the rest would have been the odd tavern, and desolate farm building. The estate was acquired in 1599 from Robert Horseman, a sitting tenant who stubbornly remained in his house near St. Mary's church, dying the following year.

There follows a steep descent down the hill to Shepherd's Bush Green. Of ancient etymology, the verdant greensward was used as a stopping off point for sheep-farmers on their way to London. The road crossed, as it still does, the northern side of this green to become what the romantic highway agencies of the twentieth century in their poetic spirit called "the A4020" - and thence to the wilder heaths of Acton, Ealing and Hanwell.

Holland House, Kensington, built in 1605, which Shakespeare would have seen on his right as he passed along Notting Hill Gate and down towards Shepherd's Bush. Painting: John Buckley 1812.

Shakespeare had now left the environs of what we now call Greater London, and had entered a wilder England... but what was this landscape like in 1596?

CHAPTER SEVEN

THE ELIZABETHAN LANDSCAPE

In the England of 1500 there were three sheep to every human being. An Italian visitor wrote: "The population of this island does not appear to me to bear any proportion to her fertility and riches."

Although enclosure had begun in a piecemeal way by the sixteenth century — though not as profoundly and wide-sweepingly as the Parliamentary enclosure of the eighteenth — vast tracts of England were still forest, heath, and common land. Even at the end of the seventeenth century Gregory King estimated that there remained three million acres of woods and coppices. The Forests of Dean, Sherwood, Arden, Epping and Wychwood covered whole counties in vast, living breathing carpets of oak and beech.

But by Shakespeare's day these ancient forests were being chipped away, gnawed at by the fuel-hungry populace; hacked down for house-building, ship-building, and chiefly iron-working, for timber was the primary fuel of Elizabethan England.

In addition to these diminishing but still gigantic forests, much of the country was heath and common - great stretches of wild moors with hardly any inhabitation except for the odd cottage. Even as late as the eighteenth century Daniel Defoe described huge parts of Surrey, Hampshire and Berkshire as "desert... barren land that lyes all together, reaching out every way in the three counties..."

Yet if we are to attempt an accurate description of the landscape through which Shakespeare passed on this August day in 1596, it is important to remember that just as today the country is as regionally varied as a country can possibly be, so was it then. As W.G. Hoskins notes in his "The Making of the English Landscape," "All over the lowlands of central England the ancient and hedgeless open fields stretched to the horizon, but in the regions towards the.... south-east, the typical landscape was one of small, hedged fields, of scattered farmsteads, and winding lanes and paths joining farm to farm."   So it must have been this kind of scene that met the playwright's eyes as his horse carried him west on this summer's morning, over Shepherd's Bush and down the highway to Acton, Ealing, Southall, Hayes and Uxbridge - a watery green dappled kaleidoscope of cottages, farms, small fields, fruit orchards, churches, manor houses, woods, and streams.... By the time he reached the Midlands north of Oxford the landscape of course would be utterly different – vaster, open, with an immense acreage of skies and the deep loneliness of distance.

The roads were by all accounts dreadful. The Elizabethans seemingly talked about little else but the condition of the highways, along with the weather. Act after Act was passed, to no avail – even in his retirement Shakespeare was adding his name to a petition to improve his county's highways; a subject clearly very close to his heart. In a statute of 1555 it was declared that "Highways are now both very noisome and tedious to travel in, and dangerous to all passengers and carriages." Floods were a common Elizabethan spectacle, making roads impassable. In A Midsummer Night's Dream the vividness of the imagery indicates it was written from the standpoint of a travelling eyewitness, probably about the notorious floods of 1594:

> *...the winds, piping to us in vain,*
> *As in revenge, have suck'd up from the sea*
> *Contagious fogs; which falling in the land*
> *Have every pelting river made so proud*
> *That they have overborne their continents:*
> *The ox hath therefore stretched his yoke in vain,*
> *The ploughman lost his sweat, and the green corn*
> *Hath in his youth attained a beard;*
> *The fold stands empty in the drowned field,*
> *And crows are fattened with the murrion flock;*
> *The nine men's morris is filled up with mud,*
> *And the quaint mazes in the wanton green*
> *For lack of tread are undistinguishable...*

A later writer, Thoresby, who died in 1715, gives a detailed account of his battle with floods in Hertfordshire: "... the rains had raised the washes upon the road near Ware to that height that passengers from London that were upon the road swam, and a poor higgler was drowned, which prevented me from travelling for many hours; yet towards evening we adventured with some country people who conducted us over the meadows, whereby we missed the deepest of the wash at Cheshunt, though we rode to the saddle-skirts for a considerable way, but got safe to Waltham Cross, where we lodged."

No floods on this August morning in 1596. For now, as Shakespeare feels the city recede behind him and the straggle of buildings peter out into hedgerow and gravel-pit, lavender field and water-mill, he can still hear the cry of boys playing in the apple orchards not far from the road, an argument in a roadside inn, the peal of girl's laughter from an upstairs room, and the chestnut plod of his mount in the honey-coloured August dust of the A4020...

CHAPTER EIGHT

MARKET GARDENS AND INNS:
ACTON & EALING

The old Irishman sits heavily on a bench in front of St. Mary's Church, sporting a leather cap at a jaunty angle. Next to him his friend is shorter, untidier. They bear a striking resemblance to the Two Ronnies about to perform a sketch.

I was in search of the old village pump of Acton – well, one must find something to do on these interminable Sundays – and when I approached the two semi-somnambulant Celts my request set off a volley of memories. It was like tossing a match into a pile of tinder. They fizzed and crackled like parched twigs and by the time I left half an hour later we were like old friends. We practically exchanged addresses.

Their memories of old Acton came thick and fast. My technique on this journey of deliberately targeting the oldest members of each community I passed through was paying off. Speaking to very old people gets you back further than you might think. For example, I who am living in 2024 have spoken to someone – my Great-Aunt in fact – whose father was born in 1866. So in one conversation I can connect with images, memories and facts of over one hundred and fifty years ago. There are only four such links in this chain that take us all the way back to Shakespeare.

Shakespeare's road west. The Uxbridge Road (A4020) looking towards Acton Vale.

For the past hour I had drifted along the Uxbridge Road. As it leaves Shepherd's Bush and becomes Acton this long, straight stretch is essentially a skeleton of Victorian parades, curlicued pubs with cream chimneypots and clutches of smokers puffing shabbily around the grimy benches – the "Queen Adelaide," the "Princess Victoria," – but fronted, the shops, with the dirty plastic signage of modern commerce, like painted whores breasting the thoroughfare with brash cries advertising their wares.

Remove the gaudy lipstick-coloured signage and underneath lies a colder, brown-grey structure of more genteel soul, of more dignity, but still slightly damp and dusty in the corners. At the edge of Shepherd's Bush Shakespeare would have crossed over Millen Bridge, a timber structure taking him over a brook across to the Uxbridge Road.

This stretch is, and was, straight as a Roman motorway, facing dead into the sun as it sets in the West. And it continues thus all the way to Uxbridge. Indeed, right from Newgate itself all the way back at the City Wall, we have travelled virtually in a straight line – evidence indeed of its Roman origin.

As you get further from London proper there are less and less Georgian buildings, and even the Victorian stock starts to thin out, replaced more frequently by 1950's council estates and 1980's office blocks, many of them empty, offering ever increasing "special rates." The road passes a huge ocean-liner Mecca Bingo Hall, and nearby, betting shops – gambling dens and cock-fighting halls for the benefit generation. Outside the general stores Asian youths share cigarettes; a grim-faced cyclist adjusts the earpiece of his ipod; old men sit on benches doing nothing, staring into the sun under the golden leaves of the plane trees of Acton Park. For centuries Acton was simply a small cluster of houses around the medieval Church of St. Mary's - which is where I met my two old Irishmen - providing refreshment for travellers on the road to Oxford, together with a smaller farming community at East Acton, and a number of scattered farm dwellings. The majority of residents were employed in agriculture on the large holdings or in the five common fields farmed in strips.

Although only five miles from London, the state of the roads in early times was such that Acton was probably a few hours travel from London, so if Shakespeare left his rooms in St. Helens at around 8 o'clock, then it would already have been around 11 o'clock when his horse ambled onto bustling Acton Green. There were many inns and taverns in the vicinity of the church of St. Mary's, so that the travellers and their beasts could take refreshment before continuing the trek up Acton Hill, or to tidy themselves up before going on to London.

Shakespeare may have stopped for a drink here or he may have pressed on. The earliest recorded inn is in 1337, and the number of inns and taverns increased over time reflecting the volume of traffic. There were numerous brooks and springs providing clean water, so the horses were well catered for. During Shakespeare's lifetime the discovery of mineral bearing springs at Acton Wells created a spa within easy reach of London, which flourished for some time, but declined as Bath and Tunbridge Wells gained favour. The relative closeness to London, yet rural nature of Acton, encouraged a number of wealthy people to build country retreats from the City, but in 1596 the locale was a sparse stopping-off point. Far in the future was Acton's reputation as a "Motor Town."

But as I pass through today, the feeling is that the great age of Acton's industrial might has faded. The Times in 1956 described it as having one of the two largest concentrations of industry south of Birmingham; the very names of the firms are redolent of a confident, New Elizabethan Britain: *Napiers (engines and vehicles), Wilkinson Sword (swords, razors, vehicles), CAV and Lucas (automobiles).*

No more... today the remnants of Acton's great industrial past – the hulking factory buildings squatting back on their huge haunches back from the main road like dinosaurs holding back from a charge and squinting in the sun – are flat conversions, or self-storage warehouses. A long, flat stretch of road takes me across what once Acton Vale; there remains little of this broad expanse save for Acton Park; opposite the park stands the "Acton Vale Club" proudly stating its affiliation with the "C.I.U." The "Sani Hotel," stands opposite Old Oak Road, where an extremely tall

Victorian pillar marks the western edge of the Vale. Old Oak road is perhaps the last remaining echo of the ancient origin of the locale; Acton is Saxon derivative of "Oak Farm."

Past Acton Park on the right stands the magnificently art deco Newman Hire Company building: *"Set Dressing for Film and Television"* in now-cracked 30's lettering, like the scratched titling of a vintage film. It is Lewis Scher House, once the Headquarters of BAFTA – an apt organisation for England's leading playwright of the age to pass. Across the road a huge Tesco Metro fronts an ocean liner of new-build apartments, all empty, the discounts getting bigger and more desperate by the day, "20% off! 30% off!" - ending with perhaps "oh, for God's sake just have them."

As Shakespeare crossed the Vale his heart would have expanded with the vista, lungs powered by sweet air, skin freshened by August sunshine tinged with an oak-laden breeze. For us, now, we are confronted by the now-familiar grey parades of Victorian houses turned into shops: the Snappy Pizza, the South China Restaurant, and – an odd anachronistic survival from a Dickensian century - "James Gilbert & Son, metalworkers, established 1867." Acton Vale is now self-storage castles, Victorian factories adorned like, yes, more painted whores, slicked with boastful swathes of coloured canvas, lowest price guaranteed.

As we reach the edge of the Vale the flatness goes and little ripples and swells return to the landscape. Somewhere way below our feet lies the Elizabethan roadway Shakespeare took – and its descendant, though caked with decades of tarmac, still rises and falls to the same dictates of contour. Past the Acton Waterhouse rock garden the land starts to rise gently. All the tributary streets to this stretch of the Uxbridge Road are echoes of its old fame as London's orchard and market garden: they are all "groves," vanished now but visible to Shakespeare as secret avenues of oak and fruit tree and leafy glade.

The road climbs past another ocean-liner's bulwarks – the Gala Bingo Hall, not far from Acton swimming baths, built in 1904. The baths are near Mill Grove Hill – where, today, alas, there is neither mill nor grove. But there is a hill. And as if to confirm the prior existence of a mill here, the Windmill pub fronts the street with a beery smell and a garish picture of – yes, a miller.

Shakespeare would have felt the breeze on these upper slopes of Acton. The ascent doesn't seem to have been great, but you have the illusion of being quite high up – the sky becomes bigger – or is it just that the buildings are lower?

I pass Acton Town Hall on the left - "Floreat Actonan," and then, just past the Belvedere pub opposite, I spot two blue plaques on the wall of an alleyway. *"The village pump erected on Thorney conduit in 1819 by the Reverend W. Antrobus stood about sixteen feet south-east of this plaque, and was removed in 1919."* A second, smaller plaque below has been added as an afterthought, but many years later: *"The pump now stands outside St. Mary's Church further up the High Street."*

Inspired, I set off in search of this remarkable pump, which seems against all odds to have survived removal and apparent abandon to re-emerge, triumphantly restored, "further up the street." I head off past the London and County Bank, now a Natwest, past an Irish pub, the Clare Inn, almost hidden by Sunday smokers, and an amusement arcade, Caesars World Amusements. Why anyone would name an amusement arcade after the titular head of the Roman Republic is anybody's guess. Is this what Julius Caesar did on his days off? Was there nothing he liked better after crushing the rebellious Germanic tribes than to pop in to his local amusement arcade and try his luck on the fruit machines?

I head past the piercingly white and blue Baptist Church – "Glory be to God in the Highest," where the congregation of largely black Londoners are spilling out onto the pavement and drifting off in loud happy clusters into the café opposite; next door to the headquarters of the Acton Labour Party, Ruskin House – and arrive at the Market Place, in front of St. Mary's Church.

There has been a market place here for more than a thousand years – and there still is. Stalls of a farmer's market buzz with all races and ages. I approach two old Irishmen sitting on a bench, who reliably inform me that the pump is yonder, right next to the church door. *"The Acton Pump replaced the Thorney conduit water troughs (1610) fed from the ancient wells."* An iron signpost opposite says "Uxbridge 10, London 5."

The old Irish fellers have lived in Acton for fifty years. Their oldest memories are seeing horses tied up outside George and Dragon in the High Street – "it used to be a coaching inn, sir, that it was. Before this market was all done up it was known as Soapsuds Island, what with all the laundries."

The George and Dragon is still there, smoke-black London brick, blackened rafters; apparently seventeenth century, but possibly a descendant of a more ancient coaching house.

Then the shorter of the Irish chaps drops a throwaway line which in one cast reaches all the way back to Shakespeare and beyond. "And the size of those old wells... you could see down 'em from the road, so you could."

I ferret for further illumination. Wells? He continues. Apparently when he was a boy he remembers seeing ancient wells being excavated when the new market place was built; he and his young mates peered down into the deep cavities and saw the medieval brick lining of the walls. "Massive they were."

And these of course are wells Shakespeare would have seen as he passed. Moreover, he probably saw the Acton housewives gathered round washing clothes, just as my Ronnie Corbett here watched the local women of the 1930's doing exactly the same thing.

According to the sign water troughs were installed in 1610, but they possibly replaced older ones, so the playwright's horse may well have drunk his fill on this hot August day in 1596. Or stopped at the George and Dragon, where he could have drunk with a Nicolas Sly who in 1604 married Elizabeth Smith and who could have supplied a template to the writer of his famous braggart in "Taming of the Shrew." This Nicolas could have been the son of a Richard Sly who grew up in nearby Harlington and who married Alice Heath in 1565.

On this hot October Sunday four hundred years later Acton market is still buzzing. The place has a scruffy seaside feel, as indeed does the whole of Acton, with its peeling white stuccoed 1930's parades, cracked facades, junk shops, craft shops, boozy pubs, cafes, drunks, beat poets, students.

It's almost saddening to leave Acton and descend into more genteel and officious Ealing. Shakespeare would have crossed over Fordhook Bridge, which according to Ogilvie in 1675 was still constructed from timber. The crossing over the ford is still evident today, but only as a hump in the road - and now we approach the environs of Ealing, with Fordhook House and Fordhook Farm on his right. These are now buried beneath a crescent of 1950's houses in Fordhook Avenue, opposite Ealing Common tube station. The Common lay to his left and the main road ahead –

beyond the Common - was straddled with inns and hostelries.

According to Ogilvie's map of 1675, there was nothing between Acton and Ealing except "pasture" on either side of the road.

Ealing is derived from the Saxon "Gillingas," recorded as a settlement in the 12th century. It was originally in the middle of a great forest to the west of London; iron-age pots have been found near Horsenden Hill. Most of what is now West Ealing was, even at the time of the map of 1777, open countryside and fields: houses in the area were only to be found at Ealing Dean, Drayton Green and Castle Bear Hill (now called Castlebar Hill).

Ealing Common now is a long dull stretch of nothingness; to Shakespeare it would have been a bracing miles ride through wild heathland before reaching the village of Ealing. In 1777 the watering-holes along this stretch of the road included the Bell on his left, then the Feathers on his right. Then the Green Man and – intriguingly – the Old Hats, on the right just past where Northfield Lane still branches south; the road to Brentford.

A census of Ealing taken in 1599 records 426 people in 85 households – by 1664 the number of houses had grown only to 116. The "Green Man" stood near a tollgate and was a carters' stopping place with stabling for over a hundred horses. Replaced with a newly built W.H. Smiths, it's now an Iceland supermarket. Its name, however, lives on in "Green Man Lane" and council estate. Alas, also long since rebuilt, the "Old Hat" - reputed to have been in existence over 400 years ago and therefore seen by Shakespeare - was the first stage-post out of London for the Oxford mail coach during the 18th century: it was rebuilt during the early 1700's, since renamed twice and again rebuilt, from "Halfway House" to today's "Broadwalk Hotel."

A pleasant stretch of Shakespeare's journey this... for even as late as the 19th century much of the land from the Uxbridge Road south to Windmill Road, east to Northfield Avenue and west to Boston Road was given over to market gardens and orchards. Along with a few streets named after varieties of apples, almost the last remaining evidence of this is old Steel's Fruit Packing Warehouse on the corner of Northfield Road and Northcroft Road. Two streams, later hidden by housing, ran southward on either side of Ealing village in the mid 19th century. The easterly one, from water in the grounds of Elm Grove, fed some small ponds in the fields east of South Ealing Road and larger ones near Clayponds Lane before flowing under Brentford High Street to the Thames. The westerly stream ran from Castlebar Hill east of Northfield Avenue to Little Ealing, where it fed ponds at Ealing Park; farther south it followed the line of Brook Road before passing under Brentford High Street and entering the Thames near Ferry Lane.

A civilised section of the highway, then - the air heavy with the scent of fruit trees, market farmers loading huge baskets with mountains of apples, donkeys wrenching laden carts from the rutted ditches. It would have lifted his heart, though Shakespeare gives us evidence that he practised a form of positive thinking when travelling, in making Autolycus sing: *"A merry heart goes all the day; a sad tires in a mile-a."*

Moving through the suburban landscape today it is only through half-closed eyes that one can descry – using more imagination than genuine sight – the vestiges of the agricultural villages of Ealing and Acton which lie hidden at the heart of the development.

By contrast, Brentford – a half-mile south of the highway along which Shakespeare was trotting – was growing at a far more rapid rate in the late sixeenth century, commercially located as it was by the Thames. Charles Nicholl in his "The Lodger – Shakespeare in Silver Street," examines the importance of the Brentford Taverns and brothels in the lives of adventurous Londoners, including Shakespeare – it was a semi-rural haven for those seeking pleasures of the flesh and the vine. Shakespeare knew several people in this "good-time town" by the river. The Three Pigeons in Brentford was owned by a colleague in the King's Men, John Lowin. Across the river in Mortlake lived another of the playwright's fellow actors, Augustine Phillips, whose house was seemingly used as a base for the company when plague necessitated they flee the city. And Christopher Mountjoy, Shakespeare's landlord when he lodged in Silver Street in 1604, owned a house in this little Tudor Brighton.

So this locale would have been very familiar to him, even though he probably made the trip to Brentford by boat.

Ealing now melts into Hanwell... what is now an unremitting sprawl were then isolated villages linked only by the Oxford-bound highway: only 73 houses in Hanwell in 1599, a mere straggle; but although Ealing now dominates Hanwell in both size, character and heritage, in the late sixteenth century it was Hanwell that was the superior village.

Across the land to his left he may have glimpsed, through trees, the towers of the great houses of Osterley, Hampton, and Strawberry Hill. No Hanwell Asylum yet, built in the nineteenth century; and no Hanwell District School, home for several years to the young and homeless Charlie Chaplin.

We are now a mere nine miles from Tyburn... although the road is rough, the land is nevertheless still civilized, a place of inns, market gardens, carters, billowing streams. England is not yet the wild, threatening place spoken of by many travellers of the age. For now at least his journey was tolerable, routine. Plodding in the realm of the known, without fear.

Yet ahead of him lay a wilderness of sorts: the crime hotspots of Elizabethan England, beyond Uxbridge – the wooded slopes of Slepersdene between Gerrards Cross and Beaconsfield where robbers lay in wait in Cut-throat Wood (still called) and where the possibility of undignified death lay at every corner...

CHAPTER NINE

THE WILDS OF SOUTHALL & HAYES

There seems no heart to Hayes. It fringes your line of vision as you pass along the A4020 like muzak, a dull grey imposition. Hayes is only there because the A4020 is there. The 1930's and 1950's shopping parades of Acton and Hanwell have a scruffy seaside charm to them but the two-mile-long straight drawl of Hayes' 1970's shops has all the appeal of drizzle. (I'm not talking about Hayes village, of course, which lies a mile south of the A4020, just the long mind-numbing stretch of road between Southall and Uxbridge).

The most exciting shop in Hayes today must be *"Signarama! – your One-stop Shop for all your Sign Needs."* Hurrah! That's a relief: whenever I've needed a sign – and let's face it, it's been a monthly occurrence since early adulthood – I've had to visit at least three different retail establishments before obtaining my complete product. Now, heavens be praised, Hayes has provided me with a one-stop sign shop.

And that's all it does provide. Still, at least there was Southall. No two parts of Greater London could be more different. Southall is like an island – you cross Ealing Common and then suddenly you enter an exotic all-day, all-night, Indian bazaar; a splendid pocket of Asia in England, with its sari stores and beautiful almond-eyed women and its stout old gentlemen crossing the road in their tight old turbans looking like fat be-gowned walnut whips.

Southall High Street is Victorian, so Shakespeare would have seen none of it; in 1596 the area was little more than a scattering of homesteads – the most notable building being Southall Manor...

The manor-house on Southall Green was built or rebuilt by Richard Awsiter in 1587. In 1547 Robert Cheeseman died holding both the manor of Southall and that of Norwood, which together passed to his daughter Anne and her husband Francis Chamberlain. Their son, Robert Chamberlain, sold the manors in 1578 to Gregory Fiennes, Lord Dacre, and his wife Anne. So it would been occupied by the Fiennes family on the day Shakespeare passed.

The house is a timber-framed structure consisting of a central hall range of two stories flanked by gabled cross-wings of unequal width. Projecting from the hall range on the entrance or west front are a two-storied porch and a two-storied bay window, both surmounted by gables. The front is of close-studded timbering, much restored. A north-east wing was added to the house in the early 17th century and part of its north front with twin gables and restored decorative framing can still be recognized. This wing was extended westward in the 18th century, the extension being later faced with imitation timbering. There are many 19th- and 20th-century alterations to the house, particularly at the rear, but two original chimneys have survived. The interior contains fireplaces and panelling of the late 16th and early 17th centuries.

So the Southall of today did not exist at all in Elizabethan times. In fact, not even its name existed – for even in Ogilvie's map of 1675 it was simply denoted by a lane leading south from the highway to "Southwold, vulgarly known as 'Southell.'" So we owe the name of Southall itself to the laziness of popular speech.

Southall Manor House, The Green, Southall, built 1587. Photographer unknown.

In contrast, we know much of what Hayes looked like in 1596, because a survey was done of the parish and its surrounding hamlets by Lord North from 1596-8. Wood End, just south of the highway to Uxbridge, had 25 houses, including 16 cottages; Hayes End had 22 houses including 7 cottages; Cotman or Hayes Town had 12 houses; and Botwell, a mere one building and one cottage. All these hamlets which straddled the main road along which Shakespeare rode had small enclosed fields around them, but there were still large open fields around the area - in 1596 there were over 1,304 acres in 11 open fields. Three of these, Broadmead Field, Greathedge Field, and Crouch Field were well over 200 acres each, and three more, Botwell West, Botwell South, and Botwell North or East fields were all over 100 acres. Almost all the land was apparently arable, and only 48 acres were definitely meadow. The various hamlets were surrounded by over 395 acres in house land and enclosures. Lammas lands within the manor were opened for common use each year, and many of the manor-court regulations dealt with hedging, ditching, cleaning, and making water courses, repairing gates and stiles, and similar measures. Cattle and horses were grazed in the open fields after the harvest, and were stinted at one animal for every three acres, and one cow and one bullock for every cottage. The appearance of other field names in the late 16th and 17th centuries - Dawley Field, Yeading Green, Yeading Bean Field, Rolls Ditch Field - suggests that the large open fields of 1598 were gradually being broken down into smaller units. Indeed, by 1600 about a third of Hayes parish had been enclosed.

On the north side of the Uxbridge Road is Park Lane, formerly Bag Lane, which in 1596 led to Frogmore Farm but which now leads to a crescent of 1950's houses called Frogmore Gardens.

Today the route through Hayes from Southall is by brutal intersection with the giant bypass that straddles the old borough like a runway focused on a massive roundabout on the A413. As Shakespeare would have crossed fields and passed orchards, so we now pass retail parks. Then it's the long drear of the road to Hayes, starring Signarama – and thence to Uxbridge.

Uxbridge seems to have possessed a huge importance to everyone in England from the earliest times – after all, the main road west out of London was called the "Uxbridge Road." Given how hugely it featured on maps from the medieval period onwards, you'd be forgiven for thinking that the town was destined to grow and develop into the country's second city, the size of Birmingham or Manchester. A brief glance at the parish registers of the late sixteenth century tells one that the population of Uxbridge was huge compared to any other towns and villages of the surrounding district; registers including a William Sly – possibly a relation of Nicolas Sly of Acton - and an Oliver Cromwell…

Yet travelling through the rather bleak mish-mash of mini-roundabouts, traffic through-ways, redbrick university, bland office-block, mall and High Street today, it's a bit of a depressing let-down. Uxbridge seems to be the town that Never Quite Made it – and what's more, like hundreds of other towns up and down the country, along the way it lost its heart in the quest for retail and commercial glory.

From the earliest times it had everything going for it. When first mentioned in the 12th century it was already an important settlement - a chapel of ease was built in the town in the early 13th century, and in 1275 Uxbridge was one of the two Middlesex townships represented in Edward I's first parliament. By the end of the 14th century Uxbridge, following the apparent decline of the hamlet at Colham, had become the major settlement in the area.

In the eighteenth and nineteenth centuries most of London's flour was produced in the Uxbridge area, and it must also have been so in prevous times, as evidenced by the number of mills and the town's key location on the route to the capital. There were also breweries in the area, the last Brewery being Harman's Brewery based in the High

Street and extending up George Street. It was still in operation up until the early sixties.

Early-14th-century surveys suggest that manorial demesne in the parish was divided almost equally between arable and pasture with smaller scattered areas of woodland.

As Shakespeare approached the outskirts of the town in 1596 he would have passed several large open fields.

The exact location of the medieval open fields is uncertain, but most of them probably lay, as did the later common fields, south of the London road and east of the Frays stream. Only two medieval fieldnames, Rye Hill Field and Alton Field, survived into the 17th century. Stretching northward from Cowley church almost to Uxbridge and bounded by Kingston Lane and Cowley Road to the east and west were more than 300 acres of open-field land known as Cowley Field.

On the clay and gravels to the north and west of the open-field area were extensive tracts of common and waste. In 1636 these were said to comprise about 360 acres, but more reliable 18th-century estimates give their area as almost 600 acres. Northolt or Uxbridge Common, which extended into Harefield parish in the north-west, and Hillingdon Heath, straddling the London road east of Hillingdon village, each contained about 200 acres. Enclosure of small parcels of waste probably proceeded steadily from the late medieval period onwards: some open-field land had been inclosed before 1636, and the process accelerated during the 17th and 18th centuries, but on the day Shakespeare passed in august 1596 it was the huge open fields that probably met his gaze – an ocean of hay.

By 1670 large areas of the parish of Hayes and Uxbridge were in grass supplying hay for the London market – an adjunct of the increase in transportation mentioned in a previous chapter.

After Uxbridge emerged as a commercial centre in the early 12th century, economic expansion and most of the recorded social activity of the parish were concentrated there. Surviving population figures suggest that as early as the 14th century settlement also was concentrated in Uxbridge. A cursory leafing through the parish registers of the late sixteenth century tell one immediately that hundreds more people were being born, getting married and dying in Uxbridge than in the surrounding parishes.

In the 1530s there were two mills, one driven by the Frays and the other by the Colne, near the Oxford road at the west end of Uxbridge. In the 17th century a water-mill at Uxbridge belonged to Stanwell manor - and two unidentified mills at Hillingdon were included in grants of Swakeleys manor in Ickenham.

Town Mill (later Frays or Mercer's) on the Frays at the west end of Uxbridge and Crouch mill, is presumably identifiable with the two 14th-century mills of the same name. Rabbs or Robbs mill (later Cowley mill), sited on the Frays stream at the junction of Cowley Road and the modern Cowley Mill Road, is first mentioned by name in 1636, although it had almost certainly been in existence since the Middle Ages. Cowley Hall mill on the Frays west of Cowley Hall, although not mentioned by name until 1733, is shown on a map of 1641. By this date the Frays river powered at least five mills–Town or Frays mill, Rabbs mill, Cowley Hall mill, Yiewsley mill, and Colham mill–and before 1746 another mill on an arm of the Colne west of Uxbridge had apparently been built.

So in his approach to Uxbridge Shakespeare would have been entering a hive of medieval and Tudor industry – the importance of the town as a hub of the English economy and transport cannot be overestimated. The road as he approached Uxbridge would have been thick with carts and pack-horses.

The name itself is derived from "Wuxen Bridge" – the Wuxen were a Saxon tribe - which was likely to have been near the bottom of Oxford Road where the "Swan and Bottle" now stands. Uxbridge is not mentioned in the Domesday Book of the 11th century, but a hundred years later the existing church, St. Margaret's, was built, which Shakespeare would have passed as he headed into town. There are two directions he may have taken at this point – down Windsor Street to join the Oxford Road at the bottom of the gentle hill, or down the present High Street. Either route would have taken him to the bridge crossing the River Colne into Buckinghamshire.

The London-Oxford road through Uxbridge was an important national route by the 14th century. In 1358 Ellis Waleys of Uxbridge and two Acton men were granted rights of pavage in Uxbridge, Acton, and elsewhere between the two towns. Stratford Bridge, carrying the Oxford road across the Pinn between Hillingdon and Uxbridge, was in existence by 1410. Navigation of the Colne as far as Uxbridge is suggested by the construction in 1419 of a wharf serving Mede mill. By 1636 the river had been bridged at a further three places between High Bridge and Yiewsley. Stratford Bridge was rebuilt as a brick bridge of three arches before 1726, so it would have been a wooden bridge Shakespesre clattered across in 1596. Frays (later Mercer's) Bridge, carrying Uxbridge High Street across the Frays stream, was in existence by 1636. It is shown on a plan of 1675 as a brick bridge with three arches. Other important 17th-century routes in the south of the parish were Royal Lane leading from Hillingdon through West Drayton to Harmondsworth, and Dawley Lane (later

Harlington Road) running south-east from Hillingdon village towards Dawley and Cranford.

These three major north-south roads were joined by a network of lanes and access ways, chief of which were Falling or Fulling (later Kingston) Lane running from Stratford Bridge to Colham Green, Porter's or Portway Lane following the Drayton parish boundary towards Dawley, and lanes linking Goulds Green, Colham Green, and Hillingdon in the east, and Yiewsley with West Drayton in the south-west. North of the London road there were, until the 20th century, only two major roads: the road to Harefield (later Park Road) which joined the London road at the east end of Uxbridge, and Long Lane running south from Ruislip and Ickenham to the London road east of Hillingdon village. Between these Vine Lane, which ran north from Hillingdon church, may also have been of some importance. Pages or Peazes Lane left the Harefield road on Uxbridge Common and entered Uxbridge at the west end. East of the Pinn a number of minor lanes, including Sweetcroft Lane and Hercies Lane, linked the hamlets of Hillingdon and Little Hillingdon and the scattered farms to the east. Except for the widening and improvement of former minor lanes, this pattern of road communications altered little until the urban developments of the 1930s.

Surveys made in the early 16th century stress the economic importance of Uxbridge. A market-house had apparently been built by 1513, and an index to the relative prosperity of the town is provided by an assessment of 1522-3 to which 153 persons in Hillingdon parish were taxed, 77 of them from Uxbridge. Describing Uxbridge in the 1530s, Leland stressed the town's dependence on its markets, fairs, and mills. By this time Uxbridge seems to have assumed its later basic pattern of a ribbon settlement of timber-framed houses straggling for ½ mile along both sides of the Oxford road from the two wooden bridges carrying the highway over the Frays and Colne streams to its junction with Blind or Woolwind Lane (later Vine Street). Other houses probably lined both sides of the Lynch and Windsor Street for some 200 yards from the plot of waste known as the Lynch Green to the junction with High Street. In 1555 three heretics from other parts of the country were burned on the Lynch Green, where a memorial was erected 400 years later. At the intersection of Windsor Street with High Street, forming then, as later, the nucleus of the town, stood the old market-house and St. Margaret's chapel, a 13th-century foundation largely rebuilt in the 15th century.

Old Windsor Street, Uxbridge, down which Shakespeare would have trotted, past St. Margaret's Church. Photo: Road Allday 2010.

Here the playwright trotted on his way home. The medieval chapel and a few surviving domestic buildings of the 15th and early 16th centuries to some extent qualify a description of the town in the 1580s as being 'of modern date'. Nearly all the existing timber-framed buildings, many of which date from the 17th century, have altered or rebuilt frontages; they include several inns and one or two groups and individual houses in High Street.

*View of Old Windsor Street from the bottom of the lane.
Photo: Brian Burke, 2009.*

Windsor Street has suffered less alteration and retains for its size a larger proportion of such buildings. Two have also survived in Cross Street, overlooking what was formerly Lynch Green.

William Battie married Sara Turner at St. Margarets in this year of 1596 when Shakespeare was travelling through. The wedding party then repaired to the Cock Inn for the reception, where the new bride and groom received a welcome surprise present. The inn belonged to Sara's Father-in-Law Robert Winstone, and there he announced that her late Uncle Rafe Turner had left the couple *"twenty pounds in money, one fine towel, two pairs of fine sheets, and a pillow."*

It is only fancy which conjures Shakespeare hearing the toast to good old Uncle Rafe as he trots past the Cock Inn down Windsor Street - but you never know.

The most notable 16th-century house in Uxbridge is the Treaty House, known as the Crown and Treaty House Inn, which stands on the south-west side of High Street between the Frays and Colne streams. It is built of brick and the principal front, lying at right angles to the road, has two two-storied bay windows with moulded brick mullions and transoms. There are three chimneystacks with clustered shafts at the rear and a curvilinear gable at the north-east end. The interior retains some original features. The present range is thought to represent little more than a single wing of the 16th-century mansion, originally the seat of the Bennet family. In 1645 the house was used for meetings between Royalist and Parliamentary representatives negotiating the abortive 'treaty' of that year; it was then clearly of considerable extent. A view published in 1789 shows the building reduced to its present size; it had two curvilinear gables above the bays on its principal front and a two-storied bay window at its north-east end. By the end of the century High Street had been diverted to run immediately past the house which at that time was let out in tenements. By 1816 the house had become the Crown Inn, an earlier 'Crown' near the market having recently been demolished.

Three surviving inns in the High Street - the 'Three Tuns', the 'King's Arms', and the 'George' - incorporate 15th- and 16th-century work. Two other inns, the 'Leg' and the 'Axe', mentioned in the 15th century, probably changed their signs during the 17th century: the 'Axe' is last mentioned by name in 1647. The 'Bull' and the 'Cross Keys' were in existence by 1548. Other Uxbridge inns mentioned before 1648 include the 'Swan', standing in 1602.

The Crown and Treaty Inn, 16th century. Shakespeare would have passed it on his left as he made his way into Buckinghamshire. Photo: Robb Emms 2007.

The pub now called "The Queens Head" has a sign depicting Anne Boleyn, wife of Henry VIII. The pub was previously called "The Axe" and possibly dates from the 1540s. A tunnel connects the pub to the church. At the bottom of Windsor Street there is a cemetery with an archway. It was here on Lunch Green that three heretics were burned to death in 1555, found guilty of denying the trinity.

Uxbridge seems to have a heritage of Catholic conspiracy, and not without relevance to Shakespeare. The Catholic priest Edmund Campion, who trained in Douai in the Netherlands, travelled England on horseback to give covert support to Catholics, giving sermons in secret and pretending to be a diamond merchant. In 1580 he came to Uxbridge and hid for a couple of weeks in a house owned by William Catesby. In 1581 Campion was caught, and hanged, drawn and quartered in London. The 40 or so Catholics who died in this period are called the "Douai martyrs" which is also the name of the local Catholic secondary school, in Ickenham. Shakespeare's father himself was a signatory to Campion's campaign, a secret document being discovered in the rafters of the house in Stratford by builders in the eighteenth century.

In 1605 the Gunpowder Plot was uncovered. The flamboyant six-foot leader, Robert Catesby, (son of William), escaped and hid in his house in Uxbridge. He was later shot.

For some centuries Uxbridge had an unsavoury reputation. The jurist William Arabin said of its residents "They will steal the very teeth out of your mouth as you walk through the streets. I know it from experience." Experience? Is he implying that he was strolling down Uxbridge High Street one afternoon when a dentally-fixated ne'er-do-well leapt out from a nearby alleyway and filched his molars?

The road out of Uxbridge into Buckinghamshire is long and straight, crossing the water-meadows of the River Colne. Here Shakespeare was entering wilder, poorer country, a land thick with woods, robbers, travelling families – and the oases of market towns huddled in valleys below the beech-covered hills of the Chilterns…

CHAPTER TEN

TRAVELLER'S REST: UXBRIDGE
TO BEACONSFIELD

In Ogilvie's map of 1675 Buckinghamshire is marked as beginning just over the River Colne as it passes through Uxbridge – and it is exactly the same today. Saxton's sixteenth century map shows that the old road Shakespeare used followed the path of the present A40 from Uxbridge all the way to West Wycombe. Compared to the road to Bath via Maidenhead Thicket - the A4 - the Oxford Road from this point was apparently very poor and difficult for wheeled traffic. Coaches were heavy and lumbering; crossing the River Colne into Denham after Uxbridge was particularly hazardous, as the land often became waterlogged.

Bulstrode Park comes up on Shakespeare's right, with its earthworks and Saxon legends. His choice of Lear and Cymbeline as subjects for his later plays point to a love of old British history as well as Tudor - his was indeed the age of the first antiquarians, those first eccentric gentlemen like Camden and Leland and Harrrison to start pottering about the weird old stone circles and ruins of ancient England. So

Shakespeare was drawn to Bulstrode – lying as it does just
he reached the common of Gerrard's Cross, and with less

*Bulstrode Park nr. Gerrards Cross ("Jarrett's Cross") – the
view Shakespeare would have seen on his left.
Photo: Andrew Smith 2006.*

hedges in his day than there are now, he would have a fine
view of the old Saxon and British Barrows and burial
chambers. The town itself – or scattered settlement as it was
then – went under the older name of Jarrett's Cross.

Redhill – the valley after Gerrards Cross – was, and is, a
steep descent, followed by a climb into Beaconsfield. This
was dangerous country. Robbers waited in the wooded
fringes of the road at both Slepersdene before Beaconsfield,
and Holtspur Heath on the other side of the town.

This part of Buckinghamshire was a crime hotspot going
way back to the fourteenth century. In 1352 John Payne
was accused of killing William the Taverner of Gloucester -
(proof, incidentally, that the current A40 was indeed the old

road West, given that it was the road of choice for a Gloucester man on his way to London). But he got off on self-defence.

From 1600-1640 unemployment, poverty and vagrancy blighted Buckinghamshire. Parish registers record people "dying on their wanderings." In 1603 Ann Butler, daughter of a London merchant, was buried on September 8th "as it was thought of the plague." And Robert Dale lost all his children - Cicely in 1600, Margaret in 1608 and John in the same year. Even in the decades before Shakespeare's journey today, Henry VIII's librarian Leland was writing that the Chilterns were "full of enclosures." Land-loss, vagrancy, resentment...

Throughout the Chiltern hills there was a long tradition of dissent – Quakerism, Methodism. On the road between Gerrards Cross and Beaconsfield Shakespeare would have passed on his right the lane to Seer Green and Jordans, the home of William Penn who as an early founder of Quakerism set sail for the New World and whose legacy built Pennsylvania. In Bucks there was deep mistrust of Anglicanism, and certainly "no return to popery." There is evidence of a general suspicion of formality in religion, and cases of civil disobedience, such as sitting on hats in church.

As he approached Beaconsfield Shakespeare must surely have been hit with the first feelings of fatigue – he had been riding for about eight hours and had covered about twenty-eight miles, proclaimed by an old milestone in the long grass at the side of the road, in a voice made faint with age and moss – "London 28 miles."

Other commentators on the life of the Bard have all fallen into the habit of saying that his journey home took him two days and that he stopped overnight in Oxford.

I don't think he did. I think he took three or more days and stopped twice or even three times - either in Beaconsfield or Wycombe, Oxford, then maybe also Chipping Norton. By recreating his travels as close as possible – whilst being aware that he would have much more difficulty than me in that I was gliding smoothly on firm tarmac whereas he would have been plodding roughly along pitted and potholed highways – I nevertheless feel hungry when he would have felt hungry, tired when he would have felt tired. The body provides its own commands, and it was commanding me to stop in Beaconsfield: simple empirical empathy.

There are other reasons for concluding he put up in Beaconsfield. From the sheer number of its inns, the town was clearly a major staging-post en route from London to Oxford. Beaconsfield was basically the Heathrow or Crewe of its day, with much more accommodation even than High Wycombe which lies five miles further on. If travellers completed about thirty miles a day, then it made perfect sense to put up at one of the splendid inns on offer.

Shakespeare's entry into Beaconsfield was by way of its broad and pleasant High Street. And the street is still here, little changed in its dimensions. But in Shakespeare's day it was a town of stables, courtyards, huge inns and scattered cottages, its wide main street welcoming a traveller from London or from the West. Three large houses surrounded the old town – Hall Barn, Gregories, and Wilton Park. Shakespeare as he ambled through would have seen Capel's House next to the church, built with the £40.00 legacy left by Richard Capel the former Rector of Beaconsfield Parish Church who died in 1500. This ancient house remains – bowed by time, pushed by gravity into a sleepy sagging.

Elizabethan cottages on Shakespeare's left as he entered Beaconsfield.
Photo: Colin Smith 2009.

The old rectory was built in 1534, itself replacing an ancient nunnery – it remains, now converted into offices. Sleek XK Jaguars and Porsche's now stand nose to wall where mares once champed at the bit waiting for their masters to emerge after prayer.

Beaconsfield had its ancient market granted in 1255, its hall surviving until 1952 when the town council decided to smash it to bits.

For Shakespeare, then, entering it, say, on a late August afternoon in 1596, Beaconsfield would have been a wide light highway bordered with generously-sized inns and smaller drinking taverns. Prior to the railway, it was merely the 4 ends, Windsor, Aylesbury, Oxford and London End. It was a friendly refuge from the dangers ahead – for Highwaymen lurked in Cut-throat Wood from Holtspur to Wooburn Moor (U-bourne – "close to the Bourne," the estuary of the River Wye).

St. Mary & All Saints Church, Beaconsfield. Photo: Sealman, 2007

Buildings still remaining in Beaconsfield that Shakespeare would have seen are… The Swan (London End), 42/44 London End, 6, Shepherd's lane, 49 London End, Storewell's Farm, and Seeley's farm. In number 1 London End there are still extant Elizabthan wall paintings of a lute player and a falconer.

During the time Shakespeare would have been passing though the town wattle and daub was being gradually replaced by the more conspicuous brick; a sign of prosperity. More often than not, though, the brick was not a replacement to the ancient wattle and daub but an addition to it, covering the old surface with a handsome and long-lasting lining.

A few years later, if Shakespeare stopped off in Beaconsfield on 20th August 1600, as well he might as the theatres were closed in London, he would have heard the bells ringing for the wedding of John Gibson and his sweetheart Catherine. Simon Lee the Rector was marrying them, and Robert Waller and James Banner were the churchwardens.

So which inn did he book himself into? For a place to stay Shakespeare was spoilt for choice. There was the Star Inn, the White Hart (beloved of G.K. Chesterton when he walked out to Beaconsfield from West London, fell in love with the town and moved here until his death); the George, the Warner (sounding like a cinema but an inn which stood until the nineteenth century near the still-standing Charles Dickens in Aylesbury End); the Kings Head, first mentioned in 1507, the Crown, first mentioned in 1487, now Burke House, an ice-white palace housing an advertising company; the Saracen's Head, named by crusaders returning from the Holy Land; the Old Swan…

And all within a space not exceeding two hundred yards. This was truly the Clapham Junction of Tudor times; a place where travellers would have got to know eachother, spent evenings drinking and conversing before setting off in opposite directions the following morning. Innkeepers and their families would have become familiar faces, met yearly, twice yearly or thrice-yearly.

Inns of course are the staple environments of Shakespeare's low comedy. He is clearly referring to one from experience - possibly in Beaconsfield - when he wrote of *'... the most villainous house in all London Road for fleas. Then we leak in your chimney and your chamber lye breeds fleas like a loach.'*

But for the most part English Inns had a good reputation: Shakespeare would have paid a penny for his bed, "in sheets wherein no man hath lodged since they came from the laundress or out of the water," according to Harrison in his "Description of England." The inns were huge places, teeming with staff: Harrison declares that some could lodge up to 200-300 people, plus their horses.

There is another possible reason for thinking Shakespeare may have stopped overnight in Beaconsfield. Amongst his "country soldiers" in the second part of "Henry IV" he names one of them Ralph Mouldy. A Mouldy family lived in Beaconsfield – a William Mouldy died here in 1576. Did the Mouldy family work in one of the Inns? Was the son a soldier, a bailiff? When he wrote the parts of the "Country Soldiers" in Henry IV, he could have been writing from life.

Behind the inns were large courtyards where traveller's horses were changed, watered, fed. These courtyards are now car-parks or strange empty wastelands, portioned, sectioned, parcelled off at the back of the offices whose workers park out front in stifling metallic rows, nose to ancient pavement in a cramped diagonal.

A commuter town now – and in the sixteenth century something similar; many of the farms around the town were leased by men who were not there, for example Robert Waller of Wilton Park – a relation of Edmund Waller the poet – who more often than not was in London. By Shakespeare's day the manorial system had gone, much of the land thrown open to grass, sheep, endless grazing, wide vistas. As Shakespeare dismounted at the back of one of the large inns, he would have looked out onto the grazing land of William and Edith Cely (Seeley's Farm, now Seeley's Road) where hundreds of sheep munched lazily in the summer sunshine, looking up at the playwright dreamily as

White Hart Inn, Beaconsfield. Photo: Colin Smith 2009.

Royal Saracen's Head, Beaconsfield. Photo: Eirian Evans 2008.

he tethered his mount and looked forward to his own dinner.

It's worth quoting this whole passage from Harrison's "Description of England," as it paints a vivid picture of what Shakespeare's arrival at his first overnight stop would have been like, in terms of both accommodation and security...

'If the traveller loose oughts whilest he abideth in the inne, the host is bound by a generall custome to restore the damage, so that there is no greater securitie anie where for trauellers than in the gretest ins of England. Their horsses in like sort are walked, dressed, and looked vnto by certeine hostelers or hired seruants, appointed at the charges of the goodman of the house, who in hope of extraordinarie reward will deale verie diligentlie after outward appeerance in this their function and calling. Herein neuerthelesse are manie of them blameworthie, in that they doo not onelie deceiue the beast oftentimes of his allowance by sundrie meanes, except their owners looke well to them; but also make such packs with slipper merchants which hunt after preie (for what place is sure from euill & wicked persons) that manie an honest man is spoiled of his goods as he trauelleth to and fro, in which feat also the counsell of the tapsters or drawers of drinke, and chamberleins is not seldome behind or wanting. Certes I beleeue not that chapman or traueller in England is robbed by the waie without the knowledge of some of them; for when he commeth into the inne, & alighteth from his horsse, the hostler forthwith is verie busie to take downe his budget or capcase in the yard from his sadle bow, which he peiseth slilie in his hand to feele the weight thereof: or if he misse of this pitch, when the ghest hath taken vp his chamber, the

chamberleine that looketh to the making of the beds, will be sure to remooue it from the place where the owner hath set it, as if it were to set it more conuenientlie some where else, whereby he getteth an inkling whether it be monie or other short wares, & therof giueth warning to such od ghests as hant the house and are of his confederacie, to the vtter vndoing of manie an honest yeoman as he iournieth by the waie. The tapster in like sort for his part dooth marke his behauiour, and what plentie of monie he draweth when he paieth the shot, to the like end: so that it shall be an hard matter to escape all their subtile practises. Some thinke it a gay matter to commit their budgets at their comming to the goodman of the house: but thereby they oft bewraie themselues. For albeit their monie be safe for the time that it is in his hands (for you shall not heare that a man is robbed in his inne) yet after their departure the host can make no warrantise of the same, sith his protection extendeth no further than the gate of his owne house: and there cannot be a surer token vnto such as prie and watch for those booties, than to see anie ghest deliuer his capcase in such maner.'

If it was the Saracen's Head he put up at, he would have been welcomed by Robert Idle and his wife, who ran the inn from 1577 to 1624. The name would have appealed to the writer, fond as he was of adjectival surnames, a hangover perhaps of his boyhood wonderment at the Miracle Plays and their characters Envy, Intemperance, Laziness.

Mrs. Idle was a strong, formidable woman of stubborn temperament. After a falling out with her husband, he changed his will and left the Inn to his cousin, another Robert Idle. But she refused to budge. Two lawyers paid her a visit, along with two churchwardens George

Grimsdale and John Newington. Still she would not yield her beloved inn. And as far as we know she stayed there until she died, a sort of Tudor Peggy Mitchell. Did Shakespeare witness one or more of the couple's blazing rows as he passed through? – as firey as Kate's and Petruchio's?

His luggage taken to his room, his face washed, the weary playwright repairs to the bar.... And in the dining-room of the inn the playwright might have drunk or chatted with John Stonall, or the Bulstrodes, or the Mouldy's.

Other local characters Shakespeare may have rubbed shoulders with include Ambrose Aldridge. The Aldridge's were a large family who were still in the area four hundred years' later – in the1960's there was still an "Aldridge's" General Store in nearby Marlow. Or he may have swapped small-talk with William Grace the local butcher – after all, Shakespeare's own Father, being a glove maker, was in an allied trade, and there is a strong probability that he would have been apprenticed for a time at least to the profession.

Or the wonderfully named Widow Dancer, who died "very old" in 1612 – she may have been propping up the bar of the Saracen's that August evening.

With his love of odd names, Shakespeare was spoilt for choice in Beaconsfield: other colourful local figures who were living at the time he passed through were a Nicholas Lack, Daniel Grime, and a John Stutter, who married Phillis Sharp in 1606. In a town of so many inns, many of the local folk would have been ostlers, harness-makers, coopers, wheelwrights and saddlers. The talk at the bar and the supper table would have been of travel, local affairs, gossip.

Shakespeare would already have had dinner at midday, probably at Acton, and in keeping with the times it would have been a large meal of several courses, mostly meat, with fruit for dessert, maybe pippins and caraway seeds.

Supper was served from five o'clock onwards. The evening meal would have been slightly smaller than the one at midday, but nevertheless lavish for our standards: here is a bill of fare for a midday meal advocated in 1587: *'The First Course; potage or stewed broth, boiled meat or stewed meat, chickens and bacon, powdered beef, pies, goose, pig, roasted beef, veal, custard. The Second Course: roasted lamb, roasted capon, roasted chickens, peahens, baked venison, tart.'* When Justice Shallow is entertaining Falstaff and his friends in Gloucestershire, he calls for a supper of *'Some pigeons, Davy, a couple of short-legged hens, a joint of mutton, and any pretty little tiny kickshaws, tell William Cook.'* ('Kickshaws' were 'quelque choses,' small sweet tarts).

Fynes Morison was a Cambridge scholar who travelled across Europe and left a record of contrasting conditions and mores; he found that the English by far ate the most meat – the Italians ate the most vegetables, salads and bread.

Pigeons were on the country menu, and probably served in Beaconsfield. That Shakespeare knew of pigeons and maybe even bred them is evidenced by Hamlet knowing the bird has no gall-bladder: *'But I am pigeon-livered and lack gall to make oppression bitter.'* His mother Mary Arden had a fine dovecot at Wilmcote, seventy-five feet in circumference, with six hundred nesting holes. The young Shakespeare on visits to his grandparents would have not only watched the birds in life but eaten them at table.

The dining-room of the inn would have been thick with tobacco smoke, with both women and men puffing on pipes. Dr. Thomas Platter of Basle travelled England in 1599 and remarked on the smoking habit: he stayed in

Beaconsfield on his way to Oxford and a round-trip to Cambridge, and noted the fineness of the town's main street.

To Platter the English considered smoking a health-giver, as well as an obvious tranquilliser – indeed, the herbalist Gerard, whose house Shakespeare passed in High Holborn, also praised its disinfectant and curative qualities. The 1590's was maybe tobacco's golden age, however, for the new King James I was to denounce the habit in a highly-prescient tirade against the wicked weed in his tract 'A Counterblast to Tobacco' of 1604, in which he attacks it as a 'custom loathsome to the eye, hateful to the nose, harmful to the brain, and dangerous to the lungs, and in the black stinking fume thereof nearest resembling the horrible Stygian smoke of the pit that is bottomless' – a perceptive appraisal which could have been written in the early twenty-first century.

Whether the saloon bar Shakespeare sat down in that evening was akin to the pit of hell is not known, but to all accounts the service would have been of a high standard, as Platter makes no complaint about any inn he stayed in on his travels, and many other foreign travellers make similar positive comments.

The playwright would have been tired. A guest at an inn had the choice of being served dinner in his room, or with the host or hostess downstairs in the public dining rooms. There is evidence that Shakespeare did both: he alludes to the quality of conversation at the dining-table when he writes – *'conversation should be pleasant without scurrility, witty without affectation, free without indecency, learned without conceitedness, novel without falsehood.'*

There is no doubt Shakespeare enjoyed banter and chat at the table, and had a fondness for and an engagement with people of all classes and levels of intelligence – even his satirical portraits are not vicious, but affectionate. So he may have lingered over supper and drunk a toast with his fellow-travellers, before retiring to bed.

'Now it is the time of night that the graves, all gaping wide, every one lets forth his sprite in the church-way paths to glide...'

If the Saracen's Head was indeed the 'most villainous house in all London Road for fleas,' then there were plenty of remedies available to Shakespeare. As he mounted the creaking stairway to his bed after eating his fill at the Idle's table, and opened the door of his room, he may well have recalled advice contained in a pamphlet written by Thomas Hill in 1581: to avoid fleas, Hill writes, *'the traveller should anoint his staff with the grease of a fox or hedgehog; this would gather all the fleas to that feast and so avert them from his own person.'* Other remedies included placing various bowlfuls of goat's blood or boiled beans around the room to attract the miniscule irritants.

Whether Shakespeare spent half an hour arranging all these various elaborate solutions to the problem of infestation prior to going to bed is not known.

What is known, however, is that as night fell over the town and he lay on his pillow listening to the night-sounds of Beaconsfield beyond his window – the bark of a dog in the distance, the bleating of a grumpy sheep in Seeley's meadow, the snort and hoof-kick of a horse in the nearby stable-yard, the croaky voice of Window Dancer as she sings, tottering back to her cottage; the raised voices of Robert Idle and his wife as they have one last row in the kitchens downstairs – as he lay under the eaves and the thatch on the plump goose-feather pillow - we do know from one of his Sonnets that Shakespeare probably found great trouble getting off to sleep...

Weary with toil, I haste me to my bed,

The dear repose for limbs with travel tired;
But then begins a journey in my head,
To work my mind when body's work's expired;
For then my thoughts (from far where I abide)
Intend a zealous pilgrimage to thee,
And keep my drooping eyelids open wide,
Looking on darkness which the blind do see;
Save that my soul's imaginary sight
Presents thy shadow to my sightless view,
Which, like a jewel hung in the ghastly night,
Makes black night beauteous and her old face new.
So thus by day my limbs, by night my mind,
For thee and for myself no quiet find.

Not for him perhaps the easy slumber of the labourer; the above poem is perhaps the first ode to insomnia. For someone to whom the flow of language came so easily, the ability to switch off that conduit was perhaps not so simple.

However well or otherwise he slept in the inn at Beaconsfield, tomorrow he would be venturing down the steep descent through Cut-Throat Wood, across Wooburn Moor into the Wye Valley, and into the town of High Wycombe. Then deeper into Buckinghamshire.

It would be a tough stretch of the journey. He was now in the Chiltern Hills – bandit country.

CHAPTER ELEVEN

BANDIT COUNTRY: HIGH
WYCOMBE TO STOKENCHURCH

In all wild parts of England lurked the danger of robbery but the Chilterns in particular apparently possessed a reputation for "lawless roads," chiefly because of the vast woods that covered its sloping valleys providing cover and refuge for criminals and highwaymen. The woods of the shire are now mainly beech, but there is evidence to suggest that the proliferation of this tree was the result of deliberate planting from the fifteenth century onwards, and that the natural tree of the region was oak. So the slopes of Cutthroat Wood as Shakespeare passed through would have been more of a mixture than today, with scrub oak offering numerous hiding-places.

Such was the county's infamy that a proverb was born – "Here if you beat a bush it's odds you'll start a thief." Indeed, speaking of Buckinghamshire, Fuller says "It was altogether unpassable in times past by reason of trees." An Italian traveller, Dante's tutor no less – one Brunetto Latini – wrote of his journey from London to Oxford three hundred years earlier than Shakespeare, "We passed through many woods, considered here as dangerous places, as they are infested with robbers, which indeed is the case with most of the roads in England. This is a circumstance connived at by the neighbouring Barons on consideration of sharing in their booty and of these robbers serving as protectors on all occasions, personally and with the whole strength of their band. However, as our company was numerous, we had less fear."

Shakespeare's road out of Beaconsfield – Wycombe End.
Photo: Eirian Evans 2008.

Shakespeare would have travelled in company – possibly armed henchmen as aforementioned, or employees of the carrier if he was journeying with a pack-train. J.W. Hale asserts that it would have been common to travel armed, so Shakespeare quite possibly fingered his sword-handle as he descended the dark road between the beeches leading from Beaconsfield to Wooburn Moor. Even today the road is still deeply shaded, the traveller plunging into a valley of death, the sides cliff-like in their steepness.

The writer would have had personal experience of the shady – crooked – side of life on the road. His First Carrier in Henry IV calls highwaymen "Nicholas' clerks," and Falstaff himself and his cronies in their thieving exploits at Gadshill represent the underbelly of the traveller's travails, with the chamberlains and the ostlers being in league with the thieves.

As Harrison notes: *"I might here speake of the excessive staues which diuerse that trauell by the waie doo carrie vpon their shoulders, whereof some are twelue or thirteene foote long, beside the pike of twelue inches: but as they are commonlie suspected of honest men to be theeues and robbers, or at the leastwise scarse true men which beare them; so by reason of this and the like suspicious weapons, the honest traueller is now inforced to ride with a case of dags at his sadle bow, or with some pretie short snapper, whereby he may deale with them further off in his owne defense, before he come within the danger of these weapons. Finallie, no man traueleth by the waie without his sword, or some such weapon, with vs; except the minister, who commonlie weareth none at all, vnlesse it be a dagger or hanger at his side. Seldome also are they or anie other waifaring men robbed, without the consent of the chamberleine, tapster or ostler where they bait & lie, who feeling at their alighting whether their capcases or budgets be of anie weight or not, by taking them downe from their sadles, or otherwise see their store in drawing of their purses, do by and by giue intimation to some one or other attendant dailie in the yard or house, or dwelling hard by, vpon such matches, whether the preie be worth the following or no. If it be for their turne, then the gentleman peraduenture is asked which waie he traueleth, and whether it please him to haue another ghest to beare him companie at supper, who rideth the same waie in the morning that he doth, or not. And thus if he admit him, or be glad of his acquaintance, the cheate is halfe wrought. And often it is seene that the new ghest shall be robbed with the old, onelie to colour out the matter and keepe him from suspicion. Sometimes when they know which waie the passenger trauelleth, they will either go before, and lie in wait for him, or else come galloping apace after, wherby they will be sure, if he ride not the stronger, to be fingering with his purse. And these are some of the policies of such shrews, or close booted gentlemen, as lie in wait for fat booties by the high waies, and which are most commonlie practised in the winter season about the feast of Christmas, when seruing men and vnthriftie gentlemen want monie to plaie at the dice and cards, lewdlie spending in such wise whatsoeuer they haue wickedlie gotten, till some of them sharplie set vpon their chevisaunces, be trussed vp in a Tiburne tippet, which happeneth vnto them commonlie before they come to middle age."*

Unlike with Marlowe or Ben Jonson we have no record that Shakespeare ever had cause to draw his sword and kill someone (following his murder of an opponent in a street-fight Jonson was spared the noose only because of his ability to recite a passage in Latin, an archaic law which forbid the "clergy" to be executed, even though he was plainly non-clerical) – and there emanates from Shakespeare's plays a temperance and a humanity which makes it very unlikely that he would be quick to rise to anger. But had he been threatened, he might well have been able to defend himself.

There is evidence to suggest that Shakespeare may have been the victim of a hold-up by the famous highwayman Gamaliel Ratsey, who was hanged in Bedford on March 26th 1605. Ratsey was born in Market Deeping in Lincolnshire, the son of a wealthy gentleman, but after returning from fighting in Ireland he took to the highways as a robber. In the custom of the time he wore a grotesque mask, though not dressing as a woman as many of them did: in 'The Alchemist' Jonson refers to "...a face cut worse than Gamaliel Ratsey's.'

Following his execution there were many ballads and pamphlets published of his exploits; he was a kind of anti-Robin Hood of his day. One of these, 'Ratsey's Ghost,' tells of his robbery of a troupe of players, whom Ratsey instructs to perform for him at an Inn, for which he pays forty shillings, only to rob the band of actors the next day. During the robbery he refers to their Hamlet as being the "second-best" he has seen, and scorns the new wealth of certain players who appear to be rising above their station by buying country houses. This could be a swipe at Shakespeare following his purchase of New Place.

And so Shakespeare, saddled up and fresh in the cool summer dawn, sets off down London End on his way out of Beaconsfield. The road begins to slope immediately, levels out for half a mile over Holtspur Heath, then plunges into darkness, not to see the light until Wooburn Moor. From the top of the hill he would have seen, on a clear bright day, the distant spire of High Wycombe church, representing a pocket of civilisation in the landscape.

The old reason for High Wycombe of course was the River Wye, a small, narrow but powerful rivulet that billows from high up in the chalklands of the Chilterns and ends in the dissolve of the Thames at Bourne End. En route it watered the Celts of Buckinghamshire and then the Romans who built a large splendid villa on what is now the Rye, a vast parkland that served in medieval times as the public meadow for grazing.

As the road emerged from Cut-throat Wood onto Wooburn Moor Shakespeare would have seen several mills along the banks of the river Wye...

Once a clean, strong river muscling its way through ancient woodlands, supple, crystal and drinkable, the Wye has now been hidden away like a guilty secret beneath supermarket car-parks, pedestrian walkways, A-roads and obscure wastelands empty but for the odd hulking rusty-red skip. A nasty thing, shoved, parcelled, channelled, disguised. Stay on the road and you lose it, even though the two run roughly parallel, for the town has buried its river like an unfeeling family would put an old relative into a home.

The River Wye still running through High Wycombe. Shakespeare's road into town ran alongside the waterway. Photo: Nigel Cox 2007.

Although it built the town, the people of Wycombe no longer have any use for the Wye. Young people throw rubbish into it; old people have forgotten where it is. The paper-mills that once groaned on its banks have been demolished – finding an echo only in the name of the smart apartment blocks with red iron balconies – "Millstream Apartments."

A less wild stretch of the River Wye as it passes across the Rye to disappear under the streets of High Wycombe. The road Shakespeare took would have been to the right of this view, along what is now an abandoned water-filled railway line. Nigel Cox 2007.

But past Loudwater village – now absorbed into the sprawl of High Wycombe, there is a hidden trackway leading down to the old river, which affords a glimpse of the waterway Shakespeare would have seen as he trotted along.

A long buried footpath gradually becomes passable, tangled with thorn-bushes strung with coke cans and KFC cups – strange fruit hanging from the prickles.

Plunging into a quieter darkness, foam smelling of cheap supermarket-brand deodorant suddenly billows from a grey concrete weir. If you pursue the river it will take you away from the acreage of waste and industry into a gully of woods, more redolent of the landscape Shakespeare would have known. Round a bend, the Wye becomes darker, more disturbing. The old river has found itself. Here you can get glimpse of what the approach to Wycombe used to be like in those far-off Tudor days. In its faster course I see the long green hair of a drowned girl.

When Shakespeare threaded his way along the highway into High Wycombe he would have passed several mills – in the Domesday Book 20 are listed as lying along the River Wye. Precisely which ones were in existence in the late sixteenth century is arguable, but we do know of three: Rye Mill, the race of which remains today, Pann Mill on the edge of the Rye opposite St. John's Abbey Hospital, which has been lovingly restored, and Ash Mill on the other side of the town on the road to West Wycombe on the present Westbourne Street, which is no more.

Now the only remaining water-mill along the banks of the Wye, Pann Mill is just one of many Shakespeare would have passed.

To enter Wycombe town centre today is to navigate roundabouts and a one-way system that protects the old High Street from traffic (in the 1970's it was the subject of a television documentary called, rather dramatically, "The Town that was Choking to Death.") For Shakespeare of course it would have presented a very different spectacle – like Beaconsfield, a wide, pleasant main street bordered with spacious inns and a wide Market Square.

It is thought that the old road through Wycombe to Oxford lay along what is now Desborough Road, south of the River Wye, but that the main thoroughfare through the market town could have been in existence by the late sixteenth century, in which case the playwright would have entered the town along its now broad High Street.

The Wycombe Shakespeare entered was a market town surrounded by satellite farms and villages from where cattle and produce would be brought. Now of course the town is a light-industrial centre that still retains, however, its medieval market.

And certain buildings in Wycombe's High Street still retain an antique charm - the old Red Lion Hotel on a balustrade of which both Benjamin Disraeli and Winston Churchill gave speeches; a few old shops around the marketplace fronting the church; the Falcon Inn, the Hobgoblin - but the dominating figures of the present sprawl are the shopping malls: the Chiltern, the Octagon, and now the Eden. *"Welcome to a new Eden,"* say the hoardings, and the populace drift away from the stern grey church to the brighter pleasures of the clothes boutiques and the jewellery stores.

High Wycombe is a strange town with a strange fate. Commentators of the past praised it for its beauty – Cobbet,

Defoe; and yet the nineteenth and twentieth centuries seem to have ruined it. It is that rare thing – an industrial town of the south which was once a market town, and yet is now both. Unlike nearby Marlow which has retained its old townscape and charm, Wycombe has been bullied, beaten and forced into submission by the power of industry and commerce – all caused, of course, by the simple fact that it is situated on an arterial route from West to East or East to West.

The Guildhall, High Wycombe, 18th century successor to one Shakespeare would have seen as he wound his way through this once-pleasant market town.

The old road to Oxford threads through the town: as Shakespeare passed through he could have glanced to his right and seen the ruins of the old Hospital of St. John – still in place today in the forecourt of the old Grammar School, the fore-runner of which the playwright would have seen. Or gazed uphill to his right and seen the ruins of an old

The Hobgoblin, High Wycombe. An Elizabethan precursor would have stood here in the late 1590's.

The Little Market House, or Shambles, opposite the Guildhall. As Shakespeare rode through in the late 16th century it would have been thronging with cattle. Photo: Colin Smith 2009.

castle and settlement from the Saxon age – the home of Queen Matilda.

In the market-place at the top of the High Street there would have been a busy shambles in front of the Falcon Inn, and he would more than likely have had to thread his horse through ambling cattle. The Parish Church of All Saints would have towered above him on his right as he wove his way round the snake-like highway and reached a more open space now called Frogmoor.

As Shakespeare trotted past Frogmoor he would have steered his horse past the lumbering cattle being driven down the lane from Hughenden. There is still a Bull Lane there in the form of a narrow alleyway on the left where farmers used to drive their cattle to the shambles, now home to a strange series of shops that sell buckets, mops and surf-boards, and boasting handwritten signs that promise to unlock your mobile 'phone.

In this Square on the right as the Oxford Road leads out of town there was once two theatres, the Palace and the Repertory; a bowling alley, and Murrays' Department Store. Now, it boasts the Chicken Cottage, a KFC, and several clothes stores. The old shoe shop that served the town for fifty years or more, closed down in 2010.

The road out of Wycombe is long and dead straight, built over the old highway by Sir Francis Dashwood, in a philanthropic gesture of public works as employment for local men. Ahead, at the end of the road stands, high on a hill, the Dashwood Mausoleum, flint-pocked, overlooking the Wye Valley and West Wycombe village like a Hammer Horror film set – which of course it was. This stretch of the highway has that straggling suburban mixture of light-industry and dull residence; a nowhere place, a place to pass – a hand car-wash, Victorian villas now AA hotels and guest-houses, a veterinary surgeon, and from somewhere the smell of freshly-sawn timber, the ghost of the town's old past. As Shakespeare passed this way there would have been bodger's cottages and workshops, old men in crabbed smocks turning chair-legs.

You can hear the river Wye running softly on the left, hidden where once it sparkled exposed. Now it runs the length of the Oxford Road all the way to elegant West Wycombe Park, ancestral home of the Dashwoods.

In the Middle Ages, the east to west highway through Wycombe was not along the A40, but was to the south of the River Wye. In fact Estynton (= East Town = Easton) Street only led to St. John's Hospital whose grounds extended as far as the River. Probably the through road from Easton St. towards Loudwater was opened towards the end of the 16th century, so it was a new road Shakespeare travelled along.

The old road from Loudwater (Lude in Domesday) to West Wycombe was along the course of Desborough Road from the Gas Works to Green Street School. In 1230 it was called Strata Dusteburg and was probably a Romano British road continuing from the Pedestal past a Roman villa at Saunderton to the Icknield. Dusteburg is a variation on Dustenberg as referred to in the Domesday Book of 1086 - The Desborough Hundreds. From a point just to the south of the present bridge over the Wye near the Police Station, the road to the east followed the line of the Dyke, past the site of the Roman Villa (destroyed by the Council when the swimming baths were built) and then probably followed Back Lane to Loudwater and Windsor. The connection to the road to Beaconsfield could have been along Glory Mill Lane (now cut off by the M40) which led to the top of White Hill. The section of road now under the Dyke was enclosed in the grounds of Loakes Manor - now Wycombe

Abbey - together with the westward section of the old road towards its crossing of St.Mary's St. Copies of a sketch map of 1596 in the County Records Office and Wycombe Library concerning land belonging to All Souls College, Oxford, near Ash Mill, refers to "a lane leading from St. Margaretts to Wikham". This map shows a building along this lane some 200 yards west of the junction with what is now Westbourne Street. Ashford considers that this is the site of St.Margaret & St.Giles Leper Hospital (St. Giles was the patron saint of lepers). This is confirmed by some excavations carried out at the Desborough Road/Avenue cross-roads where some skeletons were discovered without fingers. These were obviously lepers, and the location of the graves coincides with the position of the building on the 1596 map. So Shakespeare would have seen the leper hospital on his left as he trotted past.

To the west it is not clear where this road joined the old West Wycombe Road from Oxford Road to the Pedestal. Before Sir John Dashwood built the existing straight road, using material excavated from the caves under West Wycombe Hill, the alignment of the road to West Wycombe followed the River from Ash Mill (Westbourne Street) along Nutfield Row to the "Bird-in-Hand" public house, through the yard of V. M. Millbourn's former furniture factory to Lower Mill End, along Gillett's Lane, then through West Wycombe Park, as shown clearly on the 1st edition Ordnance Survey map. This is the road, then, Shakespeare must have used - we are now obliged of course to stick to the present A40.

As he left High Wycombe and approached the village of West Wycombe, if he had gazed a few miles north up the valley leading to Princes Risborough he would have seen the Kimble villages — Great Kimble and Little Kimble.

These villages derived from the ancient British King Cymbeline, who legend tells united the Druids to fight the Romans. The locality may have resonated for Shakespeare, and he well have passed through as he followed an alternative route at another time from Stratford to London via Banbury, Aylesbury and Risborough, then Wycombe. Aubrey does mention that he passed through "Grendon" (now Long Crendon) and his Dogberry in "Much Ado" was inspired by a local constable from the village. It would have been an area he knew anyhow from touring with the Queens' Men: Thame for example was a regular stop-off point for the theatrical troupe, with its vast broad high street and many inns. An actor in the Queen's Men was killed in Thame in the late 1580's, and they arrived one man short in Stratford a few days later, leading to conjecture that Shakespeare might well have been taken on then as a replacement.

Holinshed was indeed the source of the play 'Cymbeline,' yet the area around the Kimbles with its earthworks, its ancient Whiteleaf Cross on the commanding hill, and the discoveries of ancient coins bearing the name of the old King – all would have exercised a spell over the playwright. Part of Shakespeare's mystery – and his greatness – lies in the fact that he was both modern and conservative: he both embraced Montaigne and at the same time was sceptical of the New Science, advocating that we must still "submit to an unknown fear." His was a soul nourished by the old lore of the country, the traditional stories of the shires, and to pass through the place where Cymbeline had his camp before battling with the Romans would have had a frisson for him. The romance of the play came of course from Boccaccio, its history from Holinshed, but the sense of landscape and place permeates the drama, just as the blasted heath has such resonance in Lear.

'Kimbeline's Castle,' a mile north of the road Shakespeare travelled. Legendary site of the pre-Roman King Cymbeline – the source of his play – the fact that the ancient motte & bailey site lies near the villages of Great & Little Kimble lends credence to the legend.

At eight o'clock on a cool summer's morning when I pass through the village of West Wycombe is a silent dream of an England long gone – Crown Court, a grassy square set back from the road on the left with humble dark cottages, windows so small they are like the eyes of moles, watering cans, mossy stones. And the great oak-beamed Guildhall, bleached wood like ship's timber, graffiti in the arched entrance acceptable because of its antiquity – at what point does vandalism become historical signature? – "E.B. Smith, 1904," and, simple in its Enid Blyton jolliness, "Dick," undated but redolent of the 1930's. Nobody is called Dick nowadays.

★

West Wycombe Village. Photo: Mark Percy 2008.

Out of West Wycombe the Oxford Road becomes another long, straight trackway passing over an unnoticed – by anyone but the walker – empty stream bed, grassy and smooth, curling up to a lip of reed and thicket, the remnant of a long-gone rivulet. Sheep fat as butter graze on the vast buttercupped meadow. Far away a farmer is hammering. The road is bordered on the right by one of those old, warm, red-brick mossy walls that sit deep in the earth above a Saxon ditch.

The road takes me through hundreds of dried cracked beech nut shells as though through a child's ballpond. A red triangle tells the motorist to watch out for "Farm Traffic." There is no farm traffic in this depopulated landscape except for the silhouette of a tractor on the sign itself. Pylons have replaced trees and church spires as the dominant vertical feature of the landscape, electric tight-ropes criss-crossing the valley in huge sagging arcs. A solitary blackbird attempts the crossing. "Bullocks Farm Lane," – changed of course by a local wag to "Bollocks Farm Lane."

Big crows waddle the fields, pecking, their feathers like old cheap black suits grown shiny with overuse, the grubby clothes of tattered Victorian clerks, their Sunday pecking the avian equivalent of Sunday shopping at Tescos.

Every now and then on the A40 one becomes aware of a lane suddenly branching off from the main trunk route and an old sign peeping through an unkempt tangle of bramble: "Old Oxford Road." The natural curves and twists of these little detours prove that the great swathes of long straight highway are indeed a modern invention and that the truer, more ancient track to Oxford, in its bends and dithering, was far more in obeyance with the language of the landscape than its tunnel-visioned modern successor. An empathy with the land's contours; there is affection in the sudden unexpected lurching, carrying you into deeper greener places; allotments, odd crooked cottages, the forecourts of old petrol stations grown thick with weed; welcome diversions, like making an unscheduled stop on a bus route to pay a visit to friends.

Looking down into the valley Shakespeare rode through in the 1590's: Bullock's Farm Lane, West Wycombe. Photo: David Ellis, 2006.

161

On this particular "Old Oxford Road," – as the brasher A40 skims past Piddington and Wheeler End – Alder trees line the lane thickly. Dusty black berries, thickets thinning out to the feathery artificiality of pampas grass bringing the odd foreign touch of the suburb. Victorian villas now prove the age of this true Oxford Road – "Glendyne," Sycamore Villa."

Light industry accompanies the traveller on his way out of Piddington, golden cornfields on the right, lazy sheep on the left. Up the hill, the old Oxford Road once again slinks off into the shadows, while its younger descendant pushes on, wider, straighter. I follow the old course, because this is where Shakespeare would have ridden. While the traffic noise recedes, my silent steed plunges into a darker, quieter, abandoned oblivion. This part of the Oxford Road is called "Dashwood Hill." It is a hill Shakespeare would have climbed, and it clearly hasn't been driven along for decades – proved by the existence of an old horse-trough standing crookedly at the side of the road. Weeds in cracks. Splits in the road like scars, old skin splitting, rupturing. Steep sides, cavernous chalk outcrops, teasel, Chiltern blue butterflies, trees clinging to crumbling chalk lips with the crabby fingers of roots. An old white wall buried in romantic ivy, holding back the falling soil.

The road rejoins the buzzing A40 at the top of the hill, where Studley Green – after a straggle of neat bungalows, garden gnomes, rockeries, spiky plants encrusted with sugar – boasts "Chris's Café," a 1960's living museum: cut-glass vinegar bottles, fat round tomato ketchup holders, a faded tin sign swaying outside like a prop from a Wim Wenders film, "Typhoo Served Here," once a selling-point along a 1950's and 60's highway for thirsty lorry drivers spoilt for choice of stopping-off point. Peering through the windows of the café (closed) I am looking back in time into the world of Craven A cigarettes, stubs crushed in silver-tin ashtrays, Adam Faith on the juke-box, yellow formica, menus spelt out in crooked white plastic letters on a child's black board full of tiny holes.

Old Dashwood Hill, the old and now largely-abandoned road to Oxford a mile outside West Wycombe. Photo: Steve Daniels, 2009.

Studley Green was an auto-town, but now that the nearby motorway – M40 – has taken its traffic, it is simply going through the motions, lingering on in Sunday silence, its tea-signs swaying rustily, its tumbleweed blowing. And once upon a time long ago it was always thus, a traveller's town, with horse-trough and wayside inn with its straw for the steed and the ale for the master. But no one seems to stop here any more. It has the emptiness of a Midwestern town – a stretch of long lazy days, a sweeping of a café floor, a face at a window. For the motorway has won, and it effectively killed the A40, turning it back to something of what it was centuries ago. The golden age of the A-road is over.

163

As I travel, at more or less the pace of a horse-rider in the late sixteenth century, I am becoming more aware of precisely where Shakespeare would have stopped and why: my thirst would have been his thirst; my hunger his gnawing pains – at least, after all, we have those human pangs in common. So as the journey progresses it becomes plainly obvious exactly where he would have paused for a drink or a meal. He would have stopped at Chris's café had it been there. I would have stopped had it been open.

Just outside Studley Green – or rather, Beacon's Bottom, for the former changes imperceptibly into the latter at some point, though quite where I will leave other topographers to discern - I come across a milestone set back from the side of the road and bedded deep in long wet grass: "Oxford 19, London 35." The ancient equivalents of our massive green and blue metal signs. As this journey unfolds I come across more and more of these forgotten staging-posts – from a car you simply cannot see them. They are small as garden gnomes, made for the slow traveller, the horseman. Our speed has necessitated the enormous growth in size of our roadsigns – so that to the pedestrian or cyclist they seem huge, the lexicon of giants. Stokenchurch – Saxon for "church of sticks" – St. Peter and St. Paul, set back from the main road to the right; still with its wooden tower.

Like its neighbours Stokenchurch has been killed off by the M40. Yet even before then J.W. Hale was describing the village in 1888 as having a "deserted look; it seems created for coaches to drive through, and at the present time they are like angels' visits."

And a twist of the knife is the constant white noise of the motorway, a perpetual Niagra. Do its inhabitants notice it any more? Are they all partially deaf, speaking with an unnaturally loud bark or a Les Dawson mouthing? Like a succubus it sucks the commuters from their beds each morning, injects them into its veins.

Research tells me that the old Oxford Road, the one Shakespeare would have clip-clopped along, is now a bridleway, and that the present stretch of the A40 was constructed in 1824. But I can't find the precious bridleway. I take the road through the centre of the old village. An historian's common sense tells one that any main road would pass through the middle of villages – the notion of a bypass clearly twentieth century.

Milestone, Studley Green. Dated 1744 & located at Old Dashwood Hill, part of the original London-Oxford Road, next to Dashwood Hill, now part of the A40.
Photo: David Ellis 2006.

Aston Rowant Manor – of which Stokenchurch was part - was sold in 1528 to Thomas Unton, who also held Exchequers Manor in the parish, and the settlement between his great-grandsons Edward and Sir Henry Unton in 1589 (Cadmore End, Fingest) included both Aston Rowant and Stokenchurch Manors. Sir Henry Unton, who had assigned Stokenchurch Manor during his life to Sir Henry Poole and Nicholas Payne, died in 1596, and in the following year it was sold to John Rotherham of Great Marlow.

Barley fields to the north of Stokenchurch, and Shakespeare's view on his right as he passed through the village. Photo: Andrew Smith, 2008.

Chairmaking for the London market formed an important industry here in Stokenchurch - at each end of the village is a sawmill, and there is a windmill to the south-west - and bricks were formerly made here and still are at Cadmore End, once part of this parish. There was an annual pleasure and horse fair on 10th and 11th July in the village, to which great droves of Welsh ponies and Irish horses were formerly brought, though the number has dwindled considerably in recent years.

Wormsley House, about 2 miles to the south-west of Stokenchurch, is approached through beech woods on three sides. It has belonged to the Scrope and Fane families for more than three centuries. Lord Scrope of course found his way into Shakespeare' Henry V, as one of the treacherous aristocrats.

Collier's Lane, Stokenchurch: the road to Oxford in the sixteenth century would have looked similar. Photo: Andrew Smith 2008.

In the middle of the 16th century Water End or Waters Manor was in the possession of Bartholomew Tipping. It was afterwards acquired by the Belsons, one of the Roman Catholic families of Oxfordshire, and conveyed in 1585 by Augustine Belson and his son Robert to John Bowyer, who transferred his rights in the manor in 1590 to Robert Bowyer, who would therefore have been living in the manor on the day Shakespeare passed in 1596.

The church has a nave which dates from the latter half of the 12th century, was probably lengthened in the 15th century, and the contemporary chancel appears to have been rebuilt during the first half of the 14th century, when the north transept was first erected. In the 16th century the south porch was added and the north transept rebuilt. The communion plate includes a cup and cover paten of 1574.

Church Street, coming up on Shakespeare's right. Photo: Shaun Ferguson 2008.

On the left as the town, without announcement, simply ends, I notice on the left a house called the Old White Hart; echo of a more ancient stopping off point for the passing carts.

The road heads for Lewknor, but before it takes you there you cross a flat plain past both a Dog Rescue Centre and the headquarters of the Blue Cross, and a radio mast that resembles a giant alien from an episode of Doctor Who. The road to Christmas Common lies on the left, and a field of beautiful dark chocolate brown cattle, looming like shadows in the deepening valley on the left side of the road.

Shakespeare was now leaving wild Buckinghamshire and entering Oxfordshire. He was one shire closer to his home county...

CHAPTER TWELVE

STOKENCHURCH TO WHEATLEY

Outside Stokenchurch Shakespeare's trail becomes confused by the modern brutalism of tarmac: in short, the road system has seen a number of changes. The main London road forms a short part of Aston's western boundary; it was known as via regis or 'London Weye' in the Middle Ages and became a turnpike in 1718. At that time it passed the present Warren Farm which was the 'Drum and Plough' inn in the 18th century, but in 1824 this route was 'found inconvenient' and was diverted to the west so as to be more 'commodious to the public'. The new turnpike, which was disturnpiked in 1877, and the old turnpike are shown on an estate map of 1828. An important minor road in the 18th century, but now no longer used, branched off the main road south of Tetsworth, ran through Copcourt, along Copcourt Church Way to Aston, and then joined the highway at the foot of Aston (i.e. Stokenchurch) Hill. Copcourt Church Way had been made by order of the Bishop of Oxford in 1620.

Church Way running from Chalford Green to Aston may have been laid out at the same time. Both the Icknield Way (Akemannestrete in 1298 and Hacknall Way in 1768), at the foot of the Chilterns, and the Lower Icknield Way to the north were well-defined roads in the 18th century, but are now grass tracks. In 1958 there were three chief lines of communication, all partly ancient ones: a minor road from Postcombe to Sydenham, which has always linked the hamlets of Chalford and Kingston Stert; another minor road from Kingston Stert by Kingston Blount to the Stokenchurch road; and the road from the 'Lambert Arms' on the London road to Chinnor, which links all the villages at the foot of the Chilterns. The last used to pass close to Aston House and the village, but it was straightened, probably shortly after 1768, and made to run further to the south.

The Kingston road was also diverted: it used to enter the village from Stokenchurch close by Kingston House, but in 1835 it was made to pass west of the 'Red Lion' so as to bypass the big house, and was then continued in a straight line to Kingston Stert instead of along Pleck Lane, its former route.

We are now in Oxfordshire. There follows the long descent through Aston Wood, past the old timber yard at the foot of the hill – remembered as a boy and hardly changed except for now a modern Range Rover sits where an old green land-rover was.

But before entering the darkness of Aston Wood Shakespeare would have looked to his left from the summit of the hill and seen Shirburn Castle, nestling then as it does now in its crenellated, moated secrecy just off the road to Watlington. A medieval castle built in 1378, it lies in ruins now, allowed to fall into dilapidation by an acrimonious feud amongst members of the Macclesfield family who lived here from the early seventeenth century. The seventh Earl was evicted only a few years ago, and with his eviction came the break-up of one of the one of the finest private libraries in the world. In the seventeenth century and beyond it was a place of science and learning; the Second Earl was a member of the Royal Society, and in 2005 when his descendant was thrown out, numerous letters from Isaac Newton were found stashed away in a cupboard.

When Shakespeare passed the castle in 1596 it was occupied by the Chamberlain family.

Shirburn Castle, Oxfordshire, which Shakespeare would have seen from the Oxford Road as he descended towards Lewknor. Home of the Earls of Macclesfield. Photo Eric Dewhurst

Originally there were three drawbridges with a portcullis at the main entrance. The wide moat, doubly wide on one side, is of running water supplied from springs on the east side of the castle and also in the moat itself; Leland described the building as a 'strong pile or castlelet'. Sir Adrian Fortescue was often there after he left Stonor, and an inventory of his goods at the castle made in February 1539, a few months before his execution, throws some light on the internal arrangement of the rooms; it mentions the wardrobe, the entry, the great chamber at the lower end of the hall, the inner chamber, 'the brusshynge howse', the hall and the chamber over the parlour, and an inner chamber there; there was also a cellar, buttery, chambers each for the butler, priest, horse-keeper, cook, and chamberlains, an additional chamber, a low parlour, a kitchen larder, boulting house, fish-house, garner, brew-house, and other outhouses. From the end of the 15th century when Richard Chamberlain, his wife, and chaplain died there, to the middle of the seventeenth, the castle was lived in, at least for a part of the year by the Chamberlains, and they held it for the king during the Civil War. Today Shirburn seems like the ghost of a castle, a phantom dream of an age long gone. To walk its deserted grounds, red kites wheeling above its crumbling summer-house and orangery, the hunting lodge cobwebbed and empty, iron dog-bowls scattered and unused, the carp silent in the motionless lakes, is to be transported to C.S. Lewis's Cair Paravel in Narnia.

At the bottom of the hill the traveller is suddenly hit by a wash of sunlight, a broad expanse of vale on either side of the road, which flattens out to reach Lewknor.

The village church was founded about 1146 AD - originally known as St Mary's, now St Margaret's. It contains some late Norman work. It is built of local flint with stone dressings and comprises a chancel, nave, south aisle, porch, a north transeptal chapel and a western tower.

There are quite a few houses in the village built in flint (although some are recent imitations) but only one thatched dwelling remains (Home Farm). The road levels out on the way into Lewknor. And in the village itself the Oxford Road veers off to the right through its centre, down to the old parts near the church – Emerald Cottage, Box Tree House.

St. Margaret's Church, Lewknor, Oxfordshire. Photo: UKGeofan 2008.

Nethercote Lane, Lewknor, one of the hundreds of ancient lanes Shakespeare would have seen radiating from the main highway as he rode.
Photo: David Ellis 2006.

There were originally two inns in the village - The Old Fox (now a private house) and The Leathern Bottel which remains substantially a 16th/17th century timber-framed building with brick filling. The front yard was originally enclosed with a front wall about 5 feet high with two spaces for vehicular entrance.

*Chiltern scarp: the view Shakespeare had from Lewknor.
Photo: Simon Mortimer 2009.*

The road becomes flat and uneventful on its way from Lewknor to Tetsworth, passing Mount Farm on the right. This is open country, sparser. The Chilterns are behind us now, and with their passing the beechwoods too have gone. The skies become huge.

And yet the entry into the village of Tetsworth is gentle and rustic: it lies at the foot of a small hill sloping past tall fawn-coloured stone houses, one with a secret door set low near the bed of the lane. This house, which Shakespeare passed on his right, was at one time the most important house in Tetsworth: the manor-house. It stands now on the site of Mount Hill Farm. It was built early in the 16th century by Maximilian Petty. It is said by Wood that he pulled down the wool storage rooms attached to the 15th-century house in Thame, which he had bought from Geoffrey Dormer and where he had lived for some time. He used the materials to build his Tetsworth house. Here the Pettys lived for several generations. John Petty, grandson of Maximilian, of Tetsworth and Stoke Talmage was granted arms in 1570, and some at least of his ten children were born at Tetsworth. His son Charnell, 'an old puritan', lived at Tetsworth from 1614 to 1634, and in his will, proved 1661, willed that his wife Ellen should enjoy the mansion house. At this time it was a fair-sized house rated at 13 hearths for the tax of 1665. Plot shows it with four chimneys on his map of 1677 as he does other houses of the gentry such as Dormer's at Ascot, and Doyley's at Chislehampton. Christopher Petty sold the house in 1683 to his kinsman Christopher Wood, a relation of the antiquary Anthony Wood. Later in the century it was divided into a baker's house and three others. The present house, Mount Hill farmhouse, stands on the crown of the hill with its gable-end facing the highway and its north front facing a lane, from which it is approached by a flight of twelve steps. The gable-end has three stories and an attic; the north front has two stories and an attic. A covering of stucco mostly conceals the brick and stone of the old house, and a 19th-century porch and sash windows have been added.

Entering Tetsworth proper, there is an old forge on the left opposite the cricket green, low and whitewashed with thick black ironwork. It stands at the mouth of Silver Street, near the Old Red Lion and the billiard-smooth cricket green, familiarly called the Tetsworth Patch.

Three wagtails stalk the green studiously, like groundsmen inspecting the pitch. A swallow dives for a fly. And from beyond the fields to the left, the constant sea-wash of the motor car, on the sleeker, busier, more confident, blue, bolder M40.

The Old Forge, Tetsworth. Photo: David Hawgood 2006.

The main Oxford–High Wycombe–London road runs diagonally across this parish; it became a turnpike in 1718. The records reveal the importance of the high road in the life of Tetsworth from early times. The village is marked on a mid-14th-century road map of England, and in 1447 a licence was granted to found a hermitage at Tetsworth and a chapel of St. John the Baptist for the purpose of repairing the road. The hermit was to labour with his hands for the maintenance of the highways between Stokenchurch and Wheatley Bridge, which had long been a trouble for lack of repair. At the Reformation the hermit disappeared but he was remembered as late as the 19th century by a field called the Hermitage beside the Thame road.

In the wills of medieval inhabitants of Tetsworth and the neighbourhood bequests were constantly made for the upkeep of the highways, and postmedieval documents contain many references to travellers on the Tetsworth road. As the village was 12 miles from Oxford it became a stage on the route from London to Oxford for the postchaises and carriers, and it was there that letters from the capital for the great houses such as Rycote were left.

That the roads might be dangerous appears from occasional records. A 16th-century Star Chamber case records that an Oxford carrier, taking goods and passengers to London, was attacked at Tetsworth by four armed men. They wounded the eight occupants of his conveyance and opened valuable chests. In 1681 Viscount Latimer wrote that he had arrived safely at Oxford without encountering highwaymen, having paid a visit to Roycote whilst his coach 'baited' at Tetsworth. Another case is recorded in 1762 of a highwayman robbing one of the Oxford coaches near Tetsworth.

The heyday of the road was after the making of the turnpike in 1718 until the coming of the railways in the 1840's, when road traffic dwindled and one of the principal hostelries, the 'Swan', was partly converted into a post-office and the 'Royal Oak' was pulled down.

The chief coaching inn was the 'Swan'. In the 17th century when it was the property of the Sedley family and of Sir Charles Sedley, the dramatist, its name was changed to the 'Sedley Arms' – but by 1719 the inn had reverted to its original name.

The present building is of many dates, but the late 17th-century and 18th-century facade of chequer brick conceals a much older and rather smaller building. The original house, probably built c. 1600, consisted of a timber-framed L-shaped building of two stories and attics, with three fine brick chimneystacks at the back. The range parallel with the road probably contained the hall, with a screens passage and kitchen or buttery to the east and a staircase and parlour to the west. On the first floor is a post which shows that the walls were formerly covered with wall-paintings.

Other cottages of the same period are built partly of flint and partly of brick. The farmhouse opposite to the 'Red Lion' is a rubblestone house of 17th-century date with brick additions.

Enclosure in Tetsworth was just gathering momentum when Shakespeare was passing through in August 1596; that is not to say that it was occurring while he trotted – the quick erection of a fence here, the planting of a hedge there. But the proximity of Thame and Oxford meant a substantial market for mutton and wool. It paid to enclose, and Tetsworth's time would come in the seventeenth century when its large strip system of arable farming would give way to sheep.

The Swan at Tetsworth: an Elizabethan coaching inn on the London to Oxford road. Photo: Jonathan Billinger 2008.

All these villages I am passing through on this surly Monday morning are empty. The only people I have seen for the last twenty miles are an old man buying milk from a small general store, a woman running by in lavender jogging gear, a father cycling with his boy. Has rural England died? The further we get from London – whose villages within a thirty-miles radius seem to be mere commuter precincts – England seems to become an unpeopled place. Where once they swarmed in marketplaces or trooped to church or gathered in halls for dances or saints days, now they sit closeted inside their homes illuminated by the sodium glare of television, brains drenched with the white fuzz of drama and advert, drama and advert and newspaper and advert.

St. Giles Church, Tetsworth. Photo: Steve Daniels 2009.

Now the present route of the A40 cheats the traveller out of historical insight: it sweeps round in an arc to join the M40 by one snake, and the A418 with another - an odd 1960's straddle which connects the two western arteries. For a while I am perplexed as to which route must be the older highway Shakespeare took. A glance at the map suffices – the road to Oxford taken by the playwright must have followed the route right into the village of Wheatley. He would therefore enter Oxford more centrally than does the present A40, which curves up to Headington. The present A40 was built over an old eighteenth century highway, containing an old milestone to prove it – *"L miles from London, IIII to Oxford,"* but it is still not the old road taken by travellers in the late sixteenth century.

Wheatfields: Shakespeare's view south as he passed through Tetsworth. Photo: David Hawgood 2006.

Wheatley lies in a valley at right-angles to the river Thame; a stream once flowed through the centre of the village and had to be crossed by stepping stones, but this is now contained in a culvert and covered with a road surface which forms the High Street, where most of the shops are to be found. People have lived here since Saxon times and finds from a Saxon cemetery which was discovered in 1883 are housed in the Ashmolean. One of the main occupations for Wheatley people was stone quarrying and the stone was used for building Windsor Castle, Merton College, local cottages and ecclesiastical buildings, most of which were erected between the 13th and 18th centuries.

So as he trotted into town Shakespeare would have heard the clout of chisel on rock, the clatter of big dull iron hammers splitting the valuable stone, a worker lifting his sweaty head as the stranger passes by.

The way into Wheatley is a pleasant descent onto the water-meadows of the River Thame, as it slices neatly through the plain. Over the gently-humped bridge, the river's banks are guarded by the aching cracked backs of bent-over willows. An "old London Road" veers off to the right further along, so this would probably have been Shakespeare's way into the town – and yet there is also a road called "Roman Road" on the left, which becomes Crown Road and which – not in use as a road now but crossing fields until it reaches the houses – may have been the older entrance into Wheatley. This Crown road passes the old Crown Inn – a private house now but in its day a very large hostelry, with its huge heavy oak doors still hanging sturdily in its wide arch. Extensive stabling buildings stand opposite. This clearly hints at Crown Road being the main thoroughfare into the town – leading as it does to the High Street.

Just before the Crown, on the left hand side of the road, stands the home of *"William Mickle, poet, who wrote the 'Ballad of Cumnor Hall,' and who in this house in June 1784 entertained Johnson & Boswell."*

The old stone bridge into Wheatley that Shakespeare would have crossed.
Photo: Al Partington 2006.

The thoroughfare into the heart of the village is narrow, and would have been busy with traffic. There is evidence of its great cottage-industrial past on every corner – ancient double doors denoting workshops, old sandstone walls like bitten crunchie bars, with blackened stones at their base hinting at hearths and furnaces – Wheatley in its heyday was clearly noisy with industry. Even now there is a sense of industriousness about the town, although the old workshops have been converted into craft centres, tiny shops selling statues of Buddha, and a chapel which proclaims, rather defensively, "We do NOT believe God is a liar!" – as if the vicar is still smarting from some old accusation that has never ceased to rankle.

Quarrying stone would have been thirsty work, gallons of ale drunk at the ten public houses in the village. Shakespeare may have stopped here for a drink, so I stop at the Sun Inn on Church Road and have a roast beef dinner. My attempts at recreating his "Wheatley experience" are somewhat muted, however, when the landlady seats me in a smooth, newly decorated dining room with abstract

Crown Road, the old main road into Wheatley. Photo: Christian Guthier 2007.

paintings on the walls, and switches on a CD sound-mix from the 1980's. As I sit listening to Depech Mode and tucking in to my nouvelle-cuisine elf's portion of beef with one roast potato and half a sliced carrot, I feel further away from the sixteenth century as I have possibly ever felt in my life.

I scan the walls of the Sun Inn for any old photos, but the most ancient thing in the place is probably a 1970's painting of a fish.

Outside again, I thread my way through the quaint alleyways – its walls adorned with occasional iron-work "grips" – the thinness of which remind me of the network of crooked pathways in Cornish villages – and reach the High Street.

Wheatley was notorious for Bull-baiting and cock-fighting, sights familiar to the playwright, who had performed at the Rose on London's South Bank, itself a centre for both bloodthirsty sports. No doubt the quarry-men's meagre wages were squandered on placing bets on the unfortunate animals, so Shakespeare may have heard, on this late Summer afternoon, the cries and shouts of wagers made and the groans of wagers lost.

Other occupations in the village included faggot cutting and ochre cutting, the ochre being crushed at the windmill - which is still standing today.

Wheatley would have been the last stopping-off point before Oxford, the Elizabethan equivalent of the "Last petrol station before Newbury" - many of the inns had an upper entrance in Church Road and another in the High Street to accommodate the change of horses.

The restored Tower Mill at Wheatley, Oxfordshire. Photo: Roy Parkhouse 2007.

Half way up the narrow High Street on the left hand side stands the old Manor. Shakespeare would have seen this wonderful old house; it was enlarged and improved in 1601, and bears a plaque on the front stating "T.A. 1601", which stands for Thomas Archdale, the owner at that time. It still retains its original appearance whereas most of the other old cottages and buildings have been restored. The George coaching inn stands opposite the manor, now a private house and gift shop. Before the manor on the same side of the road lie the remains of the old Burial Ground, a medieval chapel of ease which stood there until 1795.

Outside Wheatley the road crosses Shotover Plain, a favourite haunt of highwaymen, and ascends into the great city to join the foot of Headington Hill.

No highwaymen today. And the city of Oxford approaches....

The Sun Inn, Wheatley. Photo: Roy Parkhouse 2007.

CHAPTER THIRTEEN

FRIENDS & GODSONS: OXFORD

In Oxford I don't book into the Crown Inn, which according to several anecdotes Shakespeare stopped off at on his journeys – I book into the Bell House B&B on Headington Road.

The Bell House is run by Mrs. Grindley, a middle-aged woman with loud lipstick and gravelly smoker's voice - like ninety per cent of all Bed and Breakfast proprietors in England. And like ninety per cent of all Bed and Breakfasts it's all triangular toast, shiny brass warming-pans in the unused hearth, tiny TV (colour) on a steel tray about a mile above your bed, and brochures in racks in the hall advertising Owl Sanctuaries, Butterfly Farms and coach tours of the Universities.

Shakespeare of course would have continued along with the rest of the traffic across Magdalen Bridge and on to the Golden Cross in Cornmarket where the second leg of his journey would be at an end, or the first if he had not stopped off at Beaconsfield or High Wycombe.

The playwright's feelings towards the great University town were probably ambiguous: all three of his teachers at

Stratford Grammar School – Simon Hunt, Thomas Jenkins and John Cottom – were all Oxford graduates. As a boy he had been nurtured in the art of public speaking, rhetoric, rote-learning - the stuff of actors - so he had in a strong sense been the recipient, albeit second-hand, of a traditional classical Oxford education. Yet if his plays exhibit any consistent attitude or belief at all, it is a subtle but powerful denigration of the value of the academic life: *"Not arts, nor bookes... my doctrines I derive from women's eyes."* ("Love's Labour's Lost.") And is not Hamlet the ultimate satire on the downside of a University education, producing in him not an active gentleman, outward-looking and fit for public life, but rather a dismal, introspective and powerless figure languishing in a learned helplessness?

Shakespeare's road into Oxford, over Magdalen Bridge.
Photo: James Hetherington 2008.

Shakespeare loved men of action, men who sailed close to the wind – *'banish plump Jack and banish all the world,'* – and he loved the tavern above the lecture-hall.

Whatever his feelings towards its gowned inhabitants, the town played a big part in the writer's life. A few years hence, in 1605, King James I was greeted at the gates of St. John's College by three actors dressed as Sybils, who hailed him as a descendant of the Scottish nobleman Banquo. Over the following two days the new King was in the audience of a series of learned disputations, one of which was on the topic of whether the imagination could produce actual material effects: "An imaginatio posit producere reales effectus?" The Banquo reference and the fact that Macbeth produces a dagger before him from imagination alone, steers one to the belief that Shakespeare was present at the state visit to the Oxford College. Certainly the King's Men played the city on October 9th of that same year. Perhaps it was during that visit a few weeks later that Shakespeare was told of all the Royal goings-on by his friends the Davenants, or by a Master lodging in the same rooming-house.

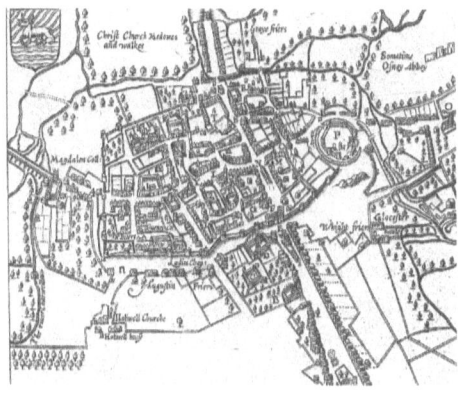

Speed's map of Oxford, 1605. Bodeleian Library.

But now, on his journey home, he dismounts gingerly. Across the road from the Golden Cross stands the Crown Inn, home of his friends the Davenants, John and Jane. He will stay here the night, eat well, converse well, and sleep well.

And so as the late afternoon sunshine melts the college towers, I set off in search of the Crown. As the road swerves right at the bottom of Headington Hill, we pass the Black Horse Coaching Inn.

The High, Oxford. Photo: Doc Searls 2007.

There is still a Crown, and it is still opposite the Golden Cross - built in 1173, still with five medieval oriel windows intact - but it is no longer an inn, simply a tavern, and it is hedged in by a big pale concrete MacDonalds that fronts Cornmarket Street.

Down the sloping alley behind the pub, I see no vestiges of Shakespeare's home from home, no Jane Davenant singing in the bar, but a small thin Polish girl with lemon streaks in her hair. For the Crown today is a dark varnished mock-Tudor carvery serving latte and lager. In the courtyard outside a knot of bald, bloated, earringed, tattooed t-shirted blokes lounge about sipping beer and rolling cigarette papers. A sign against the wall outside says that a diarist in 1667 took three days to travel from Oxford to London – I'm beginning to agree with him - before a one-day coach service was established.

The Crown Inn, Oxford, once owned by Shakespeare's friends John and Janet Davenant. Strong evidence suggests Shakespeare was godfather to their son, the poet William Davenant. Photo: R. Baxter 2010.

At the corner of Ship Street a thee-storeyed half-timbered house leans out into the street like a drunk making his presence felt by elbowing the passers-by, "hey you, listen, listen," almost overbalancing, it's ochre wattle greened by a patina of lichen-dust.

Cornmarket today is a dirty pedestrian precinct of shell-suited yahoos and teenage mums chain-smoking six inches above their newborn's crying faces, queuing up at Burger

King with their credit cards and their spots and their ipods. And weaving between them, the foreign tourists, the tanned, the relaxed, the rich.

Golden Cross Courtyard, Oxford. Opposite the Crown Inn in the Cornmarket, the Inn owned by the Davenants where Shakespeare is thought to have stayed. Postcard 1907.

Oxford is now a tourist city, a theme park where somewhere, sometime, a little studying happens – but where, you cannot see.

Shakespeare did no studying, at least none at university. He'd had enough of that at Grammar School, ten hours a day, rote-learning, accompanied by the birch. All his working life he was in battle against the university educated wits: "...not arts, nor bookes – my doctrines I derive from women's eyes." ("Love's Labours Lost.") And that ultimate advertisement for the pointlessness of the academic life, Hamlet, stumbling about miserably, inward-looking, paralysed thought, gesture without motion; between the idea and the action falls the shadow. Shakespeare preferred the lusty volition of the auto-didact.

As I sink into the pillow in my stuffy room in the Bell House, Headington Road (hot and cold running water, bathroom facilities downstairs) I think of Shakespeare lying across town in the more ample and spacious Crown. And as I drift off I muse upon what has brought me here... *and then a journey begins in my head...*

My first encounter with Shakespeare was in the Regal Cinema, Aylesbury in May 1972. The school had taken us on a trip to see Franco Zeffrelli's "Romeo and Juliet." Aged thirteen, I had just started seeing my first girlfriend, and I remember we were at that stage where our lives depended on us keeping our arms around each other at all costs (why don't adult couples walk down the road with their arms round each other?) As the lights dimmed and the seagull chatter of schoolchildren subsided I took advantage of the artificial twilight to slip my arm around the warm shoulders of the love of my life. The darkness fell, the film music swelled, the minutes passed and the story of the benighted Veronese lovers began to unfold on the screen. But I was blind to it. All I could feel was the strange, deliciously new sensation of having a girl so close I could tell what shampoo she used.

Just then a tap came on my shoulder. It was Mr. Mansbridge, the deputy head. "Save that till later, eh, Julian?" he murmured quietly, and then drew back into the shadows. I removed my arm from my girl's shoulders and we sat for the rest of the film in cold, estranged silence, staring straight ahead.

I suppose the story of Romeo and Juliet – a girl and a boy oppressed and ultimately killed by a poisonous adult stupidity – should have resonated with me that day, having fallen victim myself to an albeit far milder version of grown-up authoritarianism.

But it didn't. Like most youngsters I wondered vaguely why we were being told to learn the texts of an old sixteenth-century English writer whose characters spoke in such a strained, odd way. Why, aged fifteen, were we made to study the story of a north African soldier's insane sexual jealousy, when the only sexual jealousy we'd ever experienced was limited to feeling a certain pang of envy when Jeremy Evans got to go out with Paula Mansell?

Like most English Literature, it is of course taught far too early. When I was eighteen we studied T.S. Eliot's the Waste Land, the ultimate text of a middle-aged man's nervous breakdown. *Why?* Children's response to literature like Eliot and Shakespeare can only be factual, mechanical – the empathy comes later.

And the empathy did come. So much so that when I was twenty-one and doing a drama course in London and one of my colleagues started spouting off about how pointless it was to watch Shakespeare because his characters spoke in such a "weird way," I nearly hit him.

What had changed in the interim? Well, I had read more widely, and of course the more widely you read, the more you realise that none of these other writers - *none of them* - can even hope of coming close to Shakespeare. In fact, Shakespeare spoils you for other writers. For instance, when friends would praise someone like Steven Berkoff to the skies, my gorge would rise to the extent of wanting to commit a crime. Shakespeare of course was the first *psychological* artist in history, the first to give characters an interior life. His genius for character was sometimes at the expense of the drama itself. Hamlet, for instance, sheds the play like a carapace, discards it, and runs away. For those who think that some of Shakespeare's plays are problem plays, I think the solution lies in realising that the playwright's genius for character exceeded his time. The stage was literally not ready for his creations. Here was an unmatched psychologist whose understanding of human nature and behaviour was unerringly modern, and yet the raw material he had to work with – the stories, plots, chronicles and fables of his sources – still reeked of medievalism. Not so much problem plays, then, but evidence of Shakespeare experiencing the problem of having invented psychological drama and having to present it to an audience brought up on the mystery plays and "Gammer Gurton's Needle." His audience doubtless moved with him as the 90's progressed, but they certainly had to run fast to do so. Shakespeare outran his contemporaries, outran his audience, and outran his sources: little wonder Hamlet outran the play. It is clear that for Shakespeare, by the time he delivered his five-hour script to the playhouse, the *play* Hamlet was of subordinate interest to him than the character Hamlet. People who favour the metronome quality of the well-made pieces are admiring something other playwrights could do and have done since. People who admire the giant character plays such as Coriolanus, Richard the Third, Henry the Fourth, Hamlet, are admiring things that no other writer or artist could do at the time and, largely, since.

Outside the window Oxford slept. And across town, many years ago, Shakespeare too slumbered, a famous man among the academic nobility he had eschewed.

CHAPTER FOURTEEN

SHEEP AND FAIRS: OXFORD TO
CHIPPING NORTON

The following morning breaks cold and clear.

Outside the Bell House the air is fresh and breezy. Let us skim down Headington Hill, sweep round the Cornmarket and join Shakespeare in the soapy dawn just as he is mounting his horse and waving to Jane and John Davenant – little William his godson (and possible son) - and begin the long trot north together.

The road we both take is the Woodstock Road, passing, on the right, Canterbury Road. On the left about a mile along the Woodstock Road, stands the "Old White Horse."

The main route descends then beyond Wolvercote , crosses the Oxford Canal and the nearby railway - always a railway nearby, competition – and into Yarnton, where the "Turnpike Inn" still stands, an echo of the tollgate past. No fee for Shakespeare, though, but he may not have minded paying it to make the roads better. Almost immediately, Oxfordshire seems slightly more genuinely rustic than Buckinghamshire. The latter is a mixed county, a broth of commuters and dwindling locals. Oxfordshire seems to have more eccentrics. An old man with coloured red hair cycles past me. A Chinese woman winks at me from the pavement. Here are a slightly freer bunch of people.

A warm wind blows across the landscape.

Woodstock Road. Shakespeare headed up this highway on his way out of Oxford. Photo: Grue 2007.

The road into Yarnton, Oxfordshire. Photo: Colin Bates 2005.

Yarnton Manor, built 1580. Photo: Motacilla 2011.

St. Bartholomew's Church, Yarnton. Photo: Colin Bates 2005.

A bend in the River Thames, seen on Shakespeare's left as he rode out of Yarnton. Photo: Chris Gunns 2009.

Yarnton Bridge, that Shakespeare crossed on the road to Woodstock. Photo: Michael Van der Berghe 2005.

Begbroke is three miles on from Yarnton, with the sixteenth century inn The Royal Sun which the poet would have seen, with its quiet modest stream passing beneath, its sandy stone walls dappled by watery light. The name "Begbroke" is Anglo-Saxon for "Little Brook" and refers to Rowel Brook, a protected watercourse that runs through the village and was also the reason for its early settlement. Rowel Brook is a tributary of the River Cherwell. Begbroke is also home to the 12th century Norman church of St. Michael, St. Philip's Priory (formerly Begbroke House), Hall Farm, a Post Office, and a modern village hall with cricket and bowling greens. The former Begbroke Hill Farm, owned by the Giffard and FitzHerbert families for 500 years, is now the site of the Oxford University Begbroke Science Park.

A short way on from Begbroke is Woodstock.

Entering Woodstock is like entering a honey-coloured heaven. Its quiet streets lead you to a square of dainty shops. Shakespeare's Woodstock, of course, was pre-Blenheim Palace – there was a manor, but in a state of disrepair - but I pause at the gatehouse anyhow to see where Elizabeth was imprisoned as a princess, the manor being too dilapidated for her.

When Thomas Wyatt led an uprising in 1554 to depose Queen Mary 1st and put Princess Elizabeth on the throne in her place, Elizabeth was imprisoned in a lodge in Woodstock as a precaution, writing poetry to pass the time. There was preserved on a tablet her verses written in 1555, which Shakespeare probably saw as he passed:

> *O fortune, how thy restless, wavering state*
> *Hath fraught with cares my troubled wit!*
> *Witness this present prison whither fate*

Could bear me, and the joys I quit.
Thou causd'st the guilty to be losed
From bands wherein are innocents enclosed;
Causing me guiltless to be straight reserved,
And freeing those that death hath well deserved.
But by her envy can be nothing wrought;
So God send to my foes all they have thought.
ELIZABETH, Prisoner.

The lodge was used because the now lost Woodstock Palace or manor house was in a poor condition. A survey in 1551 reported that "the mansion... for many years past hath been decayed." She was released in April 1555 after nearly a year in captivity. Later, Elizabeth confirmed the charter that had been granted to Woodstock and gave to the town four shops and thirteen cottages. Some of the buildings still stand, and two of them are used as a public house. Woodstock also gained a weekly market on Fridays and two more fairs of four days each.

Woodstock Palace, from an old engraving. Princess Elizabeth was housed in the lodge here during Thomas Wyatt's rebellion in 1555.

At about this time glove-making was Woodstock's chief industry, one which Shakespeare knew well as his father practised the craft. Elizabethan Woodstock was also known for its polished steel work, the steel being taken from old horseshow nails. The work became very popular and fetched a high price.

The road through Woodstock. Photo: Crystalspman 2006.

The traveller to Woodstock today is met with a vision of a English country town paradise – a sort of Cotswolds version of Patrick MacGoohan's "Village" in the TV series "The Prisoner." Silver-haired retired folk drift in serene well-fed portliness past antique shops and windows fluffy and white with local linen, the scrubbed sandstone facades of tea-shop and gift-shop.

The Oxford Museum is closed, so I have a coffee in a café facing the Market Square, sipping it while the proprietor sings along to "Guitar Man." But the only words he knows to the song are the two words "guitar man," so I am treated to a professional verse, and then his low growl of "guitar man." After a couple of verses it gets a bit galling. I am tempted to join him, and then set the whole café off into a vast chorus, arms above our heads, swaying.

In front of the town hall a frizzy-haired woman is pottering about arranging flowers in huge tubs. She is wearing one of those bright yellow-green visibility jackets, with the words "Woodstock in Bloom" across it. I wonder what kind of pessimistic prescience caused some official to insist that all members of the "Woodstock in Bloom" society must at all times be clearly visible? – defence against what? A hit and run attack by members of the rival "Kidlington Crocus League?"

On the main road again out of town there stands on the right an old coaching inn, the "Marlborough Arms," now a carvery – and further down on the left, the Kings Arms Hotel, although that looks like a railway hotel.

There follows a steep descent out of Woodstock, across the River Dorn – originally travellers would have forded here, including perhaps Shakespeare.

Just over the bridge on the left there is a large, splendid, warm red-brick house sunning itself. On its front is a stone tablet proclaiming proudly but quietly that it was here, in the back garden, that one George Kempston, a tailor by trade who died in 17773, first grew the Blenheim Orange apple, which was awarded the Banksian Medal in 1822. A posthumous award, apparently. The tree was blown down in 1853 – an act of revenge perhaps by Kempston's ghost, peeved by the fact that the award for his precious apple was, quite frankly, a pretty long time coming.

Four miles out of Woodstock, the land dips in a deep valley to the right of the road. A field of thistles is shared by sheep and greasy crows. A lorry suddenly thunders by and the crows, startled, rise up from the field like black ash from a bonfire.

Seven miles out now along the Chipping Norton Road - speeding along, maybe Shakespeare broke into a trot here – and I come across another milestone. But it is so worn it is like a bar of soap that has been washed so smooth the brand name has been worn away. No mileage, no information, it stands by the side of the road dumb and useless like an old dead tooth.

I reach Enstone – a warm, lazy pocket of peace drowsing in schoolroom silence. Here was "Naboth's Vineyard" in 1876.

The church is dedicated to the murdered Kenelm, son of Kenulphus. Nearby is the Hoarstone, from which the village derives its name: Ent. being Saxon for Giant. In Shakespeare's day there may have been four stones standing upright and visible from the road – now there is only one. They possibly formed a tomb.

The landscape between Enstone and Chipping Norton opens up now – broader, vaster fields stretching out to the skyline, fields baking with corn ready to be harvested. And here now, as I pass a corner, I see a giant yellow combine harvester, where Shakespeare would have seen two dozen men and women, grinding and churning its way across the five hundred acres, regurgitating the chaff onto the dry land, doing in an hour what Shakespeare's two dozen would have taken the better part of a week.

Shakespeare was now approaching the Midlands. You can feel it in the shape of the land, in the brace of the air. The land is emptier, the fields bigger. The cosy intimacy of the south-eastern counties, with their hedges and small meadows, have been left behind. The picturesque has been sacrificed for expanse. A caravan sits in a desolate field, like a distant ship becalmed in a still sea.

The road through Church Enstone. Photo: Rob Farrow 2006.

A note must be made here of detritus. The stuff I have seen at the side of the road as I have travelled cries out to be recorded, unseen by cars of course who flash by too fast. The usual odd items of clothing, of course – a t-shirt, a shoe, which I have always found very sinister. A single shoe? Cd cases, splintered on the verge, obviously from being thrown out of a car window, the cover obliterated by rain. Evidence of the driver having suddenly been seized by an uncontrollable hatred of the music? "Right, that's it! – no more Fairport Convention! Out they go!" And weirdly, a row of video cassettes, so neatly arranged they might be on a library shelf, but here, on the edge of a wood, between a tree stump and a fence, they achieve the status of abstract art.

Most strangely and beautifully, I come across a broken necklace of pearls, scattered across the wet grass like fat droplets of dew. A lover's argument? A broken engagement?

The end of the affair? In detritus are many stories: the old mattress, the bald plastic doll, the glove.

Roadkill, of course: the rabbit flat as paper, so flat it looks like a picture of a rabbit, the skin dry and curling at the edges like crackling, sunken eyes tormented, the expression frozen in shock, tinged with a little sadness. Would Shakespeare have seen roadkill? Maybe the odd partridge caught by the wheel of a cart, a duck, chicken or rabbit struck by the hoof of an angry horse. But nothing quite so flat surely as can be achieved by the wheel of a car. He would have seen flatter remains as a boy, of course, in the workshop of his father the glove-maker - the hide of the deer pulled taut for cutting, the stretching of the two-dimensional kid.

The road into Chipping Norton. Photo: Brian Robert Marshall 2009.

Chipping Norton lies about twenty miles or so from his destination; it seems unlikely that he would stop overnight here, but may have paused in the town for a meal, or to rest and feed the horse. If he had stayed overnight at Wycombe, however, and simply stopped over for a meal at Oxford, then he may well have booked into inn for the night at Chipping Norton.

In either case, the old Stratford Road leads right through the town, so he would have passed the Wayside Cross, of which the base is still preserved – a roughened mound of stone by the town hall.

In the 1590's Chipping Norton was a major base for travellers, as was the Chapel House at Cold Norton beyond the town; in the eighteenth century a traveller described it as "a most excellent inn, and fitted up in the first style of accommodation. The Chapel had belonged to an Augustian Priory which suppressed some fifty years before Shakespeare's journeyings began. He would have seen its ruins.

In Chipping Norton itself, however, he would have found accommodation in abundance: its broad main street consisted, apparently, of little else but inns. And the town continued to be busy in the centuries following: a Lady Luxborough wrote in 1749 of the new coach service that had begun servicing travellers journeying from Birmingham to London: "It breakfasts at Henley (in Arden), and lies at Chipping Norton."

The town was described in the late nineteenth century as being one long street, and today it is not much different; what contemporary geographers describe as a "ribbon" development."

As he trotted into the wide market through Horse-Fair he would have passed "Gill & Co., Ironmongers" on the left, a sign above which reliably informs me that it was established in 1530. It stands next to the Crown and Cushion, a seventeenth century inn.

Chipping Norton is slightly shabbier than Woodstock – it's inhabitants won't mind me saying - the town seeming to lack the money that comes from having its very own palace. A rough looking woman passes by me and spits on the pavement.

I try to get dinner at 5.30pm. I can't, even though there are five pubs and about ten cafes. An Italian shakes his head sadly as he takes in his pavement-board and locks his door; a woman behind the bar of the foul-smelling "Kings Arms" laughs at me and informs me, quite proudly I feel, that "we don't do any bar food on Tuesdays." Why not? As part of some obscure religion, some Oxfordshire version of Ramadan? I ask for half a pint of the local ale, to see at any rate if I could drink something that maybe Shakespeare dank as he passed through. "We don't do the local beer," she informs me, equally proudly. Any further questions and she would probably proudly tell me that they're not actually a pub, it's all a front, an elaborate practical joke they've been playing for years.

I sit in the dark empty front parlour of the pub. Behind me, in the back yard, two women talk in low gravelly voices about how many times their mothers have married.

Escaping from the Kings Arms into the hot late afternoon sunshine, I see a blue plaque on a house near the town hall which tells any interested parties that it was "near this place," that the Reverend Stone discovered the "active ingredient of aspirin." *Near* this place? Couldn't the town council have found out exactly where? I imagined some official holding a pin above a map: "Oh sod it, it was round here somewhere."

On a bench below the town hall two young men sit in dirty track suits drinking Carling Black Label: in a few hours' time prime candidates, no doubt, for the good Reverend Stone's aspirin – if, of course, they can find out where he lives, because all they'll know is that it is "near this place."

Abandoning the Kings Arms, I repair to the Fox Inn nearby in an effort to give Chipping Norton one more chance to take me back in time to the age of the Tudors.

My wish is almost fulfilled: the bar of the Fox is low and dim, indicating the seventeenth century when as we all know people were shorter: with old photographs on the walls of nineteenth-century local figures, agricultural workers. As the gaze of the people in the photographs draws me in I become gradually aware of a small, thin man sitting opposite me, staring with large, haunted eyes. Every now and then he stands, dart a look out of the pub window – then sits back down again.

This happens three or four times. I conclude he may be waiting for someone. But he's getting up too often – it can't be that urgent.

Finally he gets up, straightens his clothing, flashes a weasel-like look at me, and says in a tight-lipped, Warwickshire brogue "sun's shining now, I can go sit outside." And he shuffles off with his pint.

He was waiting for the sun to come out. A small, dark, local man, grandson of a farmer perhaps, great-grandson maybe of one of these men pictured on the wall. Cheeks sunk, eyes wide and haunted, lifting his pint in the shadows, daily rituals observed, work in the fields, drink in the evening. Shakespeare must have shared many a tavern parlour with men like these, Andrew Aguecheeks of the streets and inns, Pistols, Nyms, Bardolphs, Falstaffs.

And here now stare their faces from the walls of this old inn in Chipping Norton – black and white images of poachers, labourers, local characters, ordinary folk but larger than life, for they'd been chosen by the photographer, who must have turned up at the town in the middle of the nineteenth century looking for people to capture on film; stopped off here at the Fox perhaps, had his subjects recommended to him – "you want to take a pitcher of old Joe mate, he'll be cummin' roond in a minnit."

And there is Joe, caught for all time: broad, weather-scarred face, grimed by a life of outdoor work, grin showing big bad teeth, features almost asiatic, cap askew, cocky smile, strong-boned, wily, son of the earth, ye good yeomen whose limbs were made in England, none of you so mean and base that hath not noble lustre in your eyes…

Stone trough on the road through Church Enstone. Photo: Alexander P. Kapp 2009.

The people Shakespeare saw and knew are all still here in these little pockets of Oxfordshire and Warwickshire, haunting the public bars, going back to their cottages with broken windows and torn scraps of coloured cloth for curtains – the odd local figures who live from hand to mouth. But they are the last of their kind, for who are their sons and grandsons in today's England? — they are the youths who lounge on public benches in the shopping precincts, sipping Strongbow, or in the doorways of closed hotels, or, the luckier, more driven ones, who go off to college to Birmingham or Leeds.

Almshouses, Chipping Norton. Photo: Peter D. Klaus, 1977.

I stay in Chipping Norton overnight on a dark rainy Tuesday, in Mrs. Harding's bed and breakfast up on the Burford Road. She is all smiles and light and fresh towels and a plate of fresh eggs and bacon in the morning. Someone once said that the further north you go, the nicer are the people.

London seems far away now. Rural England beckons. Was Shakespeare changing as he got nearer to his home county? Was he preparing a face for the faces that he met? And what were his thoughts on the wilder England he was entering?

CHAPTER FIFTEEN

ANCIENT ENGLAND: THE POET & NATURE

For Shakespeare as with all educated Elizabethans there were two natures: literary, or poetic nature, as exemplified by the pastoral - and real nature. The late sixteenth century writers both idealised and anthropomorphised the countryside: Spenser's use of landscape, for example, is purely symbolic. For Shakespeare as with every person of sensibility in the late sixteenth and early seventeenth centuries England itself was also divided into two: the urban walled city with its gates closed fast against the outside world, and the wildernesses beyond those walls. Around towns were clustered farmsteads and fields but between these places of habitation much of the country was unexplored heath, hill and forest. Nature was something to be feared: a wood was not somewhere to linger romantically, it was a place of danger to pass through as quickly as possible, usually with either weapons of your own or an armed guard.

And yet it was also an age that gave us the pastoral: Spenser's Colin Clout, the romantic shepherd in reverie, and Shakespeare's own pastoral, 'As you Like It.' Whilst accommodating these ambiguous stances, Shakespeare's attitude to nature, however, altered with his growth as a playwright – the storm in 'King Lear' is to an extent anthropomorphic, but the writer's depiction of it displays a realism hitherto unseen in English literature: with Shakespeare real landscapes, real responses to nature, were informing art.

As he was probably travelling homeward in August when the theatres were closed, the fields on either side of the highway would have been a golden abundance of corn. Nicholas Breton in his 'Fantastickes' describes the month thus: "… now begin the gleaners to follow the corn cart, and a little bread to a great deal of ale makes the travailler's dinner. The melon and the cucumber is now in request, and the oil and the vinegar to give attendance to the sallet herbs. The alehouse is more frequented than the tavern, and a fresh river is more comfortable than a fiery furnace. The bath is much visited by diseased bodies, and in the fair rivers, swimming is a sweet exercise."

Not far ahead in the calendar was the festival of 'Lammas Loaf,' the feast of first fruits, when the first grain could be made into bread. The England Shakespeare passed through would have been one of collective toil and leisure in the hot sun – whole villages occupied with field-work in preparation for a harvest festival in the ensuing weeks.

August also marked the beginning of the hunting season on fallow buck, red deer stags, and hare. Hunting was a spectacle that features often as both imagery and action in his plays, and would have been something he both witnessed and probably participated in: Titus Andronicus beckons Aaron forth with the words:

"Under the sweet shade, Aaron, let us sit, and whilst the babbling echo mocks the hounds , replying shrilly to the

well-tuned horns as if a double hunt were heard at once; let us sit down and mark their yellowing noise."

This memory of an echo seems drawn from life: that Shakespeare did depict nature thus is evidenced by the extraordinarily accurate description of the cliffs of Dover in 'King Lear.' His company visited the town while touring in October 1604 – the time he was probably writing the play, and Gloucester bids Poor Tom (really his son Edgar) to lead him to Dover:

"There is a cliff, whose high and bending head
Looks fearfully in the confined deep:
Bring me but to the very brim of it,
And I'll repair the misery thou dost bear
With something rich about me: from that place
I shall no leading need."

Shakespeare's use of nature-imagery began as metaphor but matured into what can be described as a celebratory realism, almost a nature-worship. Contrast his use of flower-imagery in an early play like King John:

To guard a title that was rich before,
To gild refined gold, to paint the lily,
To throw a perfume on the violet,
To smooth the ice, or add another hue
Unto the rainbow, or with taper-light
To seek the beauteous eye of heaven to garnish,
Is wasteful and ridiculous excess.
- King John (4.2.11-17)

- and his Archbishop of Canterbury in King Henry V:

"The strawberry grows underneath the nettle, and wholesome berries thrive and ripen best neighboured by fruit of baser quality." (Henry V, Act 1)

- with his altogether more light hearted, rapturous and photographic use of flower-imagery in the later plays such as 'Cymbeline,' –

His steeds to water at those springs
On chaliced flowers that lies;
And winking Mary-buds begin
To ope their golden eyes:
With every thing that pretty is,
My lady sweet, arise.
- Cymbeline (2.3.20-6)

- and 'The Winter's Tale,' -

Now, my fair'st friend,
I would I had some flowers o' the spring that might
Become your time of day; and yours, and yours,
That wear upon your virgin branches yet
Your maidenheads growing: O Proserpina,
For the flowers now, that frighted thou let'st fall
From Dis's waggon! daffodils,
That come before the swallow dares, and take
The winds of March with beauty; violets dim,
But sweeter than the lids of Juno's eyes
Or Cytherea's breath; pale primroses
That die unmarried, ere they can behold
Bight Phoebus in his strength--a malady
Most incident to maids; bold oxlips and
The crown imperial; lilies of all kinds,
The flower-de-luce being one! O, these I lack,

To make you garlands of, and my sweet friend,
To strew him o'er and o'er!
- The Winter's Tale" 4.4.133-50

His use of flowers in his plays is so rich and extensive (horticulturalists today even construct 'Shakespeare Gardens' containing every single flower mentioned in his works) that it cannot but betray a deep personal love of flora: their use is predominantly symbolic, but a writer's choice of symbol is crucial, and that he returns time and again in the plays to floral nomenclature is evidence that they played a powerful part in his psyche. In 'Hamlet' the playwright has Ophelia opine in her distracted, mad beauty on the power of plants:

"There's rosemary, that's for remembrance. Pray you, love, remember. And there is pansies, that's for thoughts…
… there's fennel for you, and columbine, there's rue for you, and here's some for me. We may call it herb of grace o' Sundays. O, you must wear your rue with a difference! There's a daisy. I would give you some violets, but they wither'd all when my father died. They say he made a good end."

His observation and incorporation of animals in his work is equally extensive – again, the use is not gratuitous but there to drive the play, to make the observation on character or the philosophical point – but his use of them has also been seen as remarkably accurate and drawn from life as his use of flowers: "Not only does he allude with the accuracy of a naturalist to the peculiarities and habits of certain animals, but so true to nature is he in his graphic descriptions of them that it is evident his knowledge was in a great measure acquired from his own observation." ('Folklore of Shakespeare,' T.F. Thiselton Dyer, 1883).

In all periods of history England is changing – Hardy in the late nineteenth century lamented the loss of the old agricultural ways through mechanisation – but the changes Shakespeare would have seen in the late 1590's were dominated principally by the gradual abandonment of the strip-system of farming to enclosure. The sixteenth century was the great age of the rise of the sheep-farmers and the wool industry, and for the unskilled village labourer that meant enforced idleness; leading to more and more workers on the land seeking other employment in towns.

Yet the country had not yet thrown hedges around all its agricultural land – the eighteenth century was the heyday of the fenced-off farm – and so it was still largely an open landscape he trotted though compared with the patchwork it is today. The farms Shakespeare passed on his journey were dairy, sheep, and legume, and the workers days were long: cock-crow between 3am and 5am summoned servants to their labour. If the playwright left his inn at dawn there would already have been people working in the fields. Elizabeth's Statute of Artificers detailed the working day to be from 5am to 7pm or even 8pm. Sundown spelt the end of toil. So as Shakespeare entered a village in the evening, he would have seen the men paying nine man's morris, bowls or skittles in the long shadows, and the women sitting in groups spinning or talking outside their cottages. At around midday he would have seen groups of farm-workers sitting against trees eating their midday meal – supplied by law by their employer; chiefly, pottage and ale.

The animal imagery in his plays is often fabulous and metaphorical as with his use of flowers: for example, in 'King Lear' Lord Albany speaks of the two sisters in comparison to animals; he calls them, *'Tigers, not daughters,'* and names Goneril a *'gilded serpent.'* Yet there is also much description of animals drawn from life, understandable when you consider his upbringing in a small country market town surrounded by farms, whose father was a glover and trader in wool. We have examined his obsession and love for the horse in an earlier chapter, but his mention of dogs is equally ubiquitous:

"Bulldogs are adorable, with faces like toads that have been sat on. My hounds are bred out of the Spartan kind; So flew'd, so sanded; their heads are hung with ears that sweep away the morning dew..." ('A Midsummer Night's Dream.')

- and his depictions of all things sheep are also vivid proofs of eye-witness, hands-on involvement in activities like shearing and skinning. In "The Winter's Tale" rural imagery and action abounds:

Clown

> *Let me see: every 'leven wether tods;*
> *every tod yields pound and odd shilling;*
> *fifteen hundred shorn. what comes the*
> *wool to?*

Autolycus

> *[Aside]*
> *If the springe hold, the cock's mine.*

Clown

I cannot do't without counters. Let me see; what am I to buy for our sheep-shearing feast? Three pound of sugar, five pound of currants, rice,--what will this sister of mine do with rice? But my father hath made her mistress of the feast, and she lays it on. She hath made me four and twenty nose-gays for the shearers, three-man-song-men all, and very good ones; but they are most of them means and bases; but one puritan amongst them, and he sings psalms to horn-pipes. I must have saffron to colour the warden pies; mace; dates? - none, that's out of my note; nutmegs, seven; a race or two of ginger, but that I may beg; four pound of prunes, and as many of raisins o' the sun.

This clearly is dialogue written by a man who not only witnessed sheep and wool trading first-hand, but also participated in it. Shakespeare's world was the middle-England world of corn-dealing, wool-dealing, money lending: his life as an artist was adjacent to his business life.

As a touring theatre player and as an annual (or bi-annual) commuter – and, no less importantly, an Englishman – it is unsurprising therefore to see so many references to the weather in Shakespeare's plays. Whether it is Lear's *"hurricanes,"* or Portia's metaphor *("... the quality of mercy is not strained; it droppeth like the gentle rain upon the place beneath,")*, or as more realistic backdrop in "The Tempest," – the power of meteorology is an ever-present raw material in the poet's psyche.

He must have travelled in all weathers, seen flood, tempest and storm. On occasions he must have found himself up to his horses' knees in mud – in later life he signed a petition to improve the state of the country's highways. And yet he was also content (through what Keats famously called his 'negative capability') to experience the vagaries of each season without judgement but with the poet's relish: content to see the sun glancing across the fields, flooding the land with light, and to feel the poet's rapture before nature,

At Christmas I no more desire a rose
Than wish a snow in May's new-fangled mirth;
But like of each thing that in season grows.
("Love's Labours Lost," 1.1)

When daisies pied and violets blue
And lady-smocks all silver-white
And cuckoo-buds of yellow hue
Do paint the meadows with delight...
- Love's Labours Lost" 5.2.900-4

CHAPTER SIXTEEN

WARWICKSHIRE MADE ME

Out of Chipping Norton on a bright sunny Wednesday, the rain having been blown away, the world rinsed, the streets running with gurgling channels of water, the trees decorated by cold pearls that spatter as I pass beneath in a hiss of tyre on wet road. Down through the silent early morning town, the benches emptied of youths, the horse-fair quiet, and out into the empty lanes on the way to Warwickshire.

This is the last leg of the journey. Shakespeare must have felt his hometown tugging at him; his London self draining away, his role as a family man, businessman, provider, reclaiming him. Prepare a face for the faces I will meet.

A pallor hangs over the woods as I descend the lane, then climb to the hamlet of Over Norton, past Cleevestones Farm, a big low stone building on the left, then out of Over Norton where the lane branches to the left past a field of allotments, with crooked hen-coops, a scarecrow, and a horse lifting his large head slowly as I pass, fixing me with a stare.

Steeper valleys now, as we approach Warwickshire. Broader fields, parcelled now into huge golden squares, unpeopled as then. The main Stratford Road lies to the east of the lane I am taking, because I want to take a closer look at the stone circles, the Rollright Stones as they are called, the Stonehenge of Warwickshire, which stand a few hundred yards from the highway: Shakespeare would have seen them as he passed by, but I want to examine them up close. Maybe he did.

I dismount and trudge through fields along footpaths fat with brown slugs like shiny wet cigars moving in slow motion through the corn.

I come first to the "Whispering Knights," a small group of large huddled rocks pocked by rain-holes, leaning together as though trying to protect themselves from the rain. Five upright and one flatter; old men whispering conspiratorially, *"when shall we five meet again?"* Beneath them lies a burial chamber.

There is a second, much larger circle, across the field. The Kings Men, as they are called, are a weatherbeaten ring of stones, man-size, gathered formally as though in a parliament. Both sets of stones command a vast ocean of landscape; before them, to the south, lies a descending carpet of fields and meadows stretching across Oxfordshire all the way West to Wiltshire.

I can feel the spiritual motive in the building of these structures, yet their situation and prospect – occupying as they do the best viewpoint possible within a radius of a fifty miles or more - denote a military purpose. The look-out, the gathering-place prior to attack, the focal-point, a place of safety or defense, very much like our car-parks after a fire-alarm.

Yet they also open themselves up to receiving the vast sky, the sun, the moon and the wind: primordial energies. As above, so below. And below, the crops ripen, the streams rush with fallen rain, the wheat bakes in the sun.

The 'King's Men,' the Rollright Stones on the Oxfordshire/Warwickshire border. Photo: Dennis Turner 2009.

As he trotted by on the A3400, Shakespeare would have seen these stones standing high on the hill to his left – I can see the road now snaking silvery and slippery through the trees, ribboning its way across the valley between Chipping Norton and Long Compton. There is another, solitary, stone in a nearby field about fifty yards away, the "King's Stone," a taller, yet twisted shape – like a nobleman turning to flee. As the playwright passed by each year and looked up at these stones, is it fanciful to think that the small group resemble a coven of witches, the single stone a King-to-be chancing across them on a ride across country after battle? Imagery burned itself into his subconscious daily, stored for later use.

Magic is in the air now. Shakespeare of course was steeped in the thing: it suffuses the work. His nature was an admixture of beliefs and faiths – ranging from a deep love of old Catholic England to a black pessimistic atheism – yet one strand in his soul is undoubtedly an English paganism nourished by a knowledge of folkore, magic and the rituals of the seasons.

The 'King's Stone.' Photo: Duncan Grey 2008.

This road from Chipping Norton through Long Compton must have felt to Shakespeare like the home-stretch. Warwickshire stretched out before him. The night's rain has rinsed the countryside. It sparkles in the sun.

Down the long valley, then, into Long Compton, past honey coloured houses and thatch, the old lych-gate at the church of St. Peter and Paul, its small warped brown door like a slab of chocolate. The gate itself is all that remains of a row of old cottages which Shakespeare would have passed; artisans homes, where chairs were made, iron struck.

★

*Shakespeare's view as he descended towards Long Compton.
Photo: Alan Simkins 2006.*

So the clang of hammer and the rasp of saw would have met his ears as he clopped slowly through on that summer morning of August 1st 1596. And the church itself is a sandstone beauty with a neat path cutting through neater sentries of globed privet.

He would also have seen an old malthouse on the right as he travelled through the village, next to what is now an abandoned garage. Closed down from the 1950's, its rusty pump still shows the faded ghost of a plump Michelin man waving through a coating of dust and time.

And that is Long Compton – with more rows of thatched cottages sitting like teapots and butter-dishes at the golden roadsides as the road leads us out northwards. This is a busy road now - lorries murder the village silence and scream and whine as they change gear to climb the hill. So it must have been in the late sixteenth century – Stratford was a vortex of trade, and Shipston: with their broad market squares and swarming customers for everything from wool to chairs to spices to mutton to fruit, the road would have been choked with carts.

*Church of St. Peter & Paul, and lych-gate, Long Compton.
Photo: Jennifer Luther Thomas 2006.*

On the edge of the village is a house called "The Old Dog Inn," – yet another residence converted from an ancient stopping place for travellers. Old Engand was truly a country of motels, of overnight stops, just as America is today. Nowadays we can get from one end of the country to the other in a single journey, but then it was the unloading of the luggage, the evening meal in a strange inn, the strange bed – a vast industry of catering and accommodation.

On the road out of Long Compton there are fields of corn on the left, and high fields of sheep on the left: black-faced. A lorry suddenly flashes past and the sheep, startled, rear back from the hedge.

Thomas Newton, a traveller from the eighteenth century who published his "Tour in England and Scotland" in 1785, described the country between Long Compton and Shipston-on-Stour thus: "The intervening country is open, exposed, and not very rich.... It is deficient in planting, which in course of time would generate warmth to the atmosphere, and convert the various influences of the heavens into a nutritive vegetable mould that would eventually enrich it."

Village Green, Barton-on-the-Heath. Photo: David Stowell 2006.

Two miles to the west is Barton-on-the-Heath, a small parish two miles from Long Compton to the west of the main Stratford to Oxford road about twelve miles from

Stratford. The village is mentioned by Shakespeare in The Taming of the Shrew – *'...old Sly's son of Burton Heath...'* – and it possesses a family connection in that Edmund Lambert married Shakespeare's Aunt, Joan Arden, in the 1550's, in Barton church. As a young boy Shakespeare probably visited the town, garnering memories of family occasions and perhaps absorbing a template for the Falstaffian Sly from the antics and high speech of an Uncle...

At the top of the hill as it levels out on the way to Shipston, the golden gateway to the manor of Weston Grange shimmers into view in the sunlight. We are in Manor country now, the houses of the fabulously rich sheep farmers of ancient Warwickshire, who gradually edged out the aristocrats from their Norman strongholds, the new men of the bright, thrusting Elizabethan age.

Barton House, Barton-on-the-Heath ("old Sly's son of Burton Heath"- 'Taming of the Shrew'). Photo: David Stowell 2006.

The A3400 will take us all the way to Stratford now. It follows the River Stour, the villages and towns growing up on its banks: Shipston, Tredington, Newbold, Alderminster – names that would have been as familiar to Shakespeare as the names of relatives or the poetry that was drummed into him – literally, with the birch – at school.

Hay harvest near Barton. Shakespeare was entering the wealthy farmlands of Warwickshire. Photo: David Stowell 2006.

I pass through the small village of Wolford with its manor and sixteenth century inn – but Shakespeare would never have stopped here so close as he was to home: so without pausing I carry on the road to Shipston.

Shipston itself is a broad, pleasant town with a large, generous market square and bustling shops. On my way into the town a black and white beamed coaching inn, the Horseshoe, sags to my right, now a pub.

View towards Shipston-on-Stour. Photo: David Stowell 2006.

In 1888 J.W. Hale describes the town as being "situated on a somewhat bleak upland. A quiet place in these days, but once, as is shown by the inns which still abound, lively enough with coaches and traffic. They gape in vain now, the yard gates, except haply at market day and at the mop-fair; and the horns that once made the old streets ring are blown, if blown at all, on the banks of the Styx, no longer of the Stour."

This somewhat gloomy portrait of a small town could have been ascribed to it being in the grips of the late nineteenth century agricultural depression, were it not that a century earlier the traveller Thomas Newton offered a similarly dark view: "In this bleak ill-cultivated track, the lower class of the labouring poor, who have very little other employment in winter than thrashing out corn, are much distressed for the want of fuel, and think it economy to lie much in bed, to save both firing and provisions."

Today, however, I am happy to report that Shipston has managed to extricate itself from its reputation for being the most depressing town south of Scunthorpe; I find the people bright and happy. Here in Warwickshire the folk seem to sparkle, their voices are richer, their natures more open than their grumpier southern cousins.

The contrast with Chipping Norton is stark. That town seemed on the verge of depression, yet there is a more carefree atmosphere here in Shipston. There are the usual teashops and jewellery shops and tiny shops selling knitwear that you never see anyone actually wearing, ever, and the usual happy relaxed clusters of serene retired people, ham-pink, beige-clothed, floating from antique shop to Somerfield store in poodle-haired contentment.

Shipstone High Street. Photo: Colin Craig 2009.

As the night's rain rinsed the countryside, so it has washed the town. The houses in Shipston are all clean cream, lobster pink, lime-green, birds-egg blue. Small windows reflect the sunlight like crystal. There is a mixture here of brick houses and Cotswold stone – a pale gold Natwest, a hair salon, a sixteenth century house of sun-bleached oak beam, now a Tandoori Cottage; the church of St. Michael's on the right.

Again the road leads upwards out of town; these are river settlements, so the ways out are up out of valleys, always up: the next village, Tredington, is a long row of thatched houses and a thatched inn, Tredington House, another church, with a Norman doorway.

A local joke in Stratford was the perennial "neediness" of the rectors at Tredington. The Reverend John Ward, sometime vicar of Stratford (1662-79), wrote that "I have often heard Mr. Trap say that the parsons of Tredington were always needy. One Dr. Brett, who was parson before Dr. Smith, married a Mr. Hicks; and Mr. Hicks, in a vapour, laid a handful of gold and silver upon the book; and he took it all. Whereupon Mr. Hicks went to him, and told him of it that he did not intend to have given him all; it was about ten pound. Says he, 'I want, and I will pay thee again;' but never did."

Manor Farmhouse, Tredington. Photo: Philip Halling 2008.

235

Between Tredington and Newbold, near the turn-off for Lower Eatington, there was once a doggerel-bearing sign:

"6 miles to Shakespeare's Town whose name
Is known throughout the earth
To Shipton 4, whose lesser fame
Boasts no such poet's birth."

- doggerel perhaps, but evidence of the swelling fame, the nascent tourism, the pride…

The momentum of the journey seems to be increasing the closer we get to Stratford – like reading a book, you turn the pages quicker as the last chapter approaches: outside Tredington the increased traffic load has meant that the road has been widened, a roundabout added; a big new filling station, and – oddly – across the way, a "Drive-in Barber." Was it here in 1596? – did Shakespeare take advantage of the roadside hairdresser to get his beard trimmed for Anne just before he arrived home?

Before Newbold, there is a Mill Lane on the right – a mill he would have seen. Malt was one of the biggest industries of Stratford – turning the grain into the ingredients of ale or beer: in an age of dubious fresh water, beer was drunk all day every day. It was an industry Shakespeare himself was involved in.

A White Hart Inn is still there, on the right of the main drag. The fact that this stretch of road was turnpiked indicates that it must have been incredibly busy, requiring maintenance – this was a major trade route. The local parish also wanted to cash in on the heavy traffic thundering through their villages.

A green lane approaching Newbold-on-Stour. The road Shakespeare took would have looked much the same. Photo: David Stowell 2006.

On Newbold Green, just before the old turnpike house on the left, stands an ancient thatched "hut," with beams so old the ends of the wooden pegs are frayed like chewed pencils. The hut is used currently as a shed for the green's groundsman, but after making inquiries in the local shop, an old woman tells me that it was "part of the old turnpike, dear." She is so old she may very well remember the turnpike, but I think the building is much older than the eighteenth century.

From now on Shakespeare would be encountering people he knew, familiar faces, local farmers he would have known as a child in Stratford Market place, where his father would have had a stall every Thursday morning.

The descent out of Newbold is through blue sky and sunlight – Alderminster approaches, Ettington Park House looming through tall pine trees on the right like a fairy castle, or Hogwarts: it is now, of course, Ettington Park Hotel.

River Stour: Shakespeare's view on his left as he rode through Newbold. Photo: David Stowell 2006.

Talton Mill outside Alderminster; and on the left hand side of the road now there is a steep descent which broadens out into vast water-meadows cropped short into a green crew-cut by sheep, and rutted by the veins of streams. This is land belonging to Alderminster Farm – still there, a group of low old houses to the left: houses Shakespeare would have seen. The land is open now almost to the horizon; the approach to Stratford is bright lime green, big skies.

Levelling out, the road passes Alscot Park House. Three Japanese tourists stand by the roadside near the huge gatehouse of the manor, eating yoghurt. They smile and wave at me as I glide by.

On the left about half a mile on, Monks Barn, a long low thatched - well, barn. B & B now, grain storehouse for the monks of Alderminster in Shakespeare's day. He may well have seen the brothers tilling the fields in their robes as he ambled past on his steed.

And now, almost suddenly, he is nearly home.

CHAPTER SEVENTEEN

STRATFORD: HEARTH AND HOME

The road leading into Stratford, this Shipston Road, is long and straight and gently descending into the river valley of the Avon; it converges with the Banbury Road only at Clopton Bridge in the town, but for a mile or so it passes a long suburban straddle of new-build homes, clean new estates, a giant brown sign telling us where Anne Hathaway's Cottage is, and, as one gets closer, pale grey Victorian villas. What would Shakespeare have felt, had he seen, four hundred years after his death, a huge sign pointing out the whereabouts of his wife's childhood home?

Entering Stratford today one could be passing through the suburb of any tourist town in England; the cricket club on the left, the out-of-town car-park; the butterfly farm, Alveston Manor on the right. But suddenly, at the bottom of the Shipston Road, there is Clopton Bridge, and the old market town bursts into life. On this August morning it's jammed with tourists and traffic, but the shape of the ancient town is there nevertheless: the old bridge, the wide Avon and the wider High Street leading up to the market place.

Today, kids frolic in boats under the spans of the bridge as they must have done across the centuries, as indeed the boy Shakepeare must have. The smell of cooking steak wafts warmly from hotel kitchens.

Shakespeare would have been tired as he crossed over the bridge - that sudden fatigue which is the body, adrenalin drained, saying rest now, be still. Maybe he glanced down to see the stone that he himself supplied when the structure was fortified following damages caused by a storm in the early 1590's. The bridge is much the same as it was then, a single lane forcing oncoming traffic to pause, its right side fringed now with Victorian ironwork but the same bridge nevertheless. As I cross it I find it hard to believe that such a structure, built as it was for horses and carts, can withstand the almighty load of unceasing cars and lorries.

Shakespeare would have crossed over the bridge and made his way up the hill of Bridge Street to where Henley Street bears slightly to the right. On the north bank of the bridge, had he been riding today, he would have seen his own statue, the famous group of bronze figures designed by Ronald Gowers - the poet himself at the centre, surrounded by figures of Hamlet, Lady Macbeth, Falstaff, Prince Hal. *"I am not only witty in myself, but am the cause of wit in other men."*

There are building works all around, the stutter of pneumatic drills, hoardings, dust. The bronze Shakespeare stares across at a fairground on a patch of green near the river's edge: a merry-go-round swirls. Hamlet stares forever at Yorick's skull as a woman stands nearby eating an ice-cream. Across the road there is a shop called *"Shakespearience."* On the side of a green skip in the building site someone has spray-painted the words *"cut to the chase."*

Cut to the chase... A fitting coda to this journey – and perhaps a fitting motto for Shakespeare's work. For although his friend and protégé Ben Jonson intimated that the elder playwright overwrote, one can also say that Shakespeare invented the dramatic need for action in a story. Watching or reading his plays is like jumping into a strong tide; you swim with the action. There are no eddies or millponds. He cut to the chase throughout.

Up Bridge Street, heaving, past the Marks and Spencers, Greggs, Orange 'phone shop. Then bear right into Henley Street.

And there, on the right, imposing but not grand, his home and birthplace...

Shakespeare's Birthplace, Henley Street, Stratford-on-Avon. Photo: JLC Walker 2007.

It's discreet colour has not changed in four hundred years – pale wattle, pale oak beams, its two storeys ample and prosperous but never ostentatious. His home. As you face it, three small doors are at the front, one on the right hand side of the house and the other two close together beneath a porch on the left. The middle door still has, oddly, the number "15" on it in old black iron letters. There are four sets of downstairs windows, four sets of first storey windows, and three upper storey windows. It is a large house, and it needed to be. In 1596, its occupants were Anne Shakespeare, her daughters Susanna and Judith, Williams' parents John and Mary, and maybe one or more of his three brothers Edmund, Richard and Gilbert. And perhaps also his sister Joan. So with William, that would total ten. A bustling house indeed to enter on a late August afternoon. As he approaches Shakespeare makes a mental note to look for a new larger property in the coming weeks.

At the top of Henley Street there is now a bronze statue of a jester by James Butler. In the streets roundabout there is a quote for every shop: above a WH Smiths in the High Street, "Come and take choice from my library, and there beguile thy sorrow," (Titus Andronicus); in the Garrick Inn opposite, a scrubbed American in flip-flops squints at the menu of chalked specials.

To ease the family congestion, and to make a visible statement of his growing prosperity and success, within twelve months he will have bought New Place, a few yards from the Guildhall in Chapel Lane, a stone's throw from his old school. He'll be happier there, happier than perhaps he's ever been, away from the limelight, tending his garden, planting his mulberry tree, dabbling in local land speculations, being near his beloved daughter Susanna, his wayward Judith, the lost, unhappy twin. Following his probable semi-retirement in 1612 he will spend the remainder of his years making investments, consolidating his finances, succumbing occasionally to the request for dramatic collaboration with the younger playwright

Fletcher. But he had effectively turned his back on the stage as far as being its most creative force was concerned.

Maybe he was always thus: simply a clever provincial businessman who felt most at home debating the future cost of land and cornmeal with his local friends; a middle-class aspirational burgher like his father who happened to sense, as a young man, that he was possessed of a giant poetic soul, a literary genius that he could not suppress.

Shakespeare's birthplace from the rear, and garden. Photo: Michelle Walz Eriksson 2006.

New Place is now just a garden – the house was demolished in 1759 because the owner was fed up with swarming literary pilgrims. Its close proximity to his old School and Chapel is startling: they are next door to each other. What makes a man buy a house right next door to his old school? An impulse perhaps to say to the world – look, this is how far I have come, here is my beginning and my end. Or look, this is where I began, I was formed and shaped by this place, without it I would still be working in my father's glover's shop, I owe everything to the masters who drove Latin and literature into me day after day after day until it suffused my whole being, until poetry became part of my hard-wiring, my soul, my blood, my bone and my tongue.

(The site of) William Shakespeare's final place of residence, Chapel St. He bought the house, known as New Place, in 1597 for £60, and moved in around 1610, living there till his death in 1616. The house was the second largest in Stratford, and the only house to be made of brick at the time. It was demolished in the 18th century.

In the garden of New Place children skip and frolic, just as his grand-daughter would have done; in this garden where he probably died, two drunks rant and bark over two cans of Black Label lager beneath a statue of Shakespeare who sits between figures of the two goddesses Muse and Genius. Beneath it are the words *"We shall not see his like again."*

From this garden Shakespeare must have heard the boys singing from the Guild Chapel across the road, just as he himself had sung years before. Inside, the Chapel is empty - few tourists seem to know of its relevance to the poet's life, preferring to swarm round the more famous birthplace and funerary monument in Holy Trinity church. Here in these pews the schoolboy prayed and sung.

The Guild Chapel & Grammar School, Stratford. Photo: Green Lane 2010.

The Doom painting is visible now above the chancel, ghostly and patchy from restoration centuries after Shakespeare's father himself was instructed to cover it with whitewash.

On the day of his funeral the poet's coffin would have been carried from New Place, down Chapel Street past the Guildhall and schoolroom, then left down Church Street, past Hall Croft on the left where he must have spent many happy days in the company of his daughter Susanna and her husband Dr. John Hall - through the lych-gate of Holy Trinity at the bottom of the lane, to be interred beneath the chancel of his parish church.

Above his tomb Stratford town council describe him as the "English Socrates, the English Aeschylus." The townsfolk knew what strange genius dwelt in their midst, in the guise of the gentle-natured ordinary local businessman to whom they chatted in the marketplace on Thursday mornings.

Holy Trinity Church, Stratford. Photo: Jeremy Bolwell 2010.

But that is all twenty years hence, for now on this summer evening in 1596 he dismounts outside his home in Henley Street and says goodbye to his horse which has carried him faithfully so far and whom Greenaway's man leads off now to stabling, food and rest. He has been spotted from the window by his children, young Judith running to him needily, the elder Susanna standing apart, calm yet affectionate, marking the changes in her father's features; his elderly father, still toiling in his workshop at the front of the house, glancing up from his cutting. William will tell him this evening of his application for a coat of arms lodged with the Sergeant at Arms and in a few weeks time father and son will make the journey to London together to receive it. Hamnet, his only son, is sickly and lies in bed upstairs. And hearing the noise from the garden behind, his wife Anne. She is laying out linen on tenter-hooks, hears voices from the road, makes her way round the side of the house, sees the boy bringing her husband's leather bags in and then the face of her husband himself, eyes meeting hers.

Anne Hathaway: his Anne who *"drove his Hate-away"* and saved his life. The lover of his young foolish years and the mother of his children, who maybe resented this stage-struck man who had to leave her in order to make his fortune, feed his daemon, this driven man who for all selfishness never failed to provide for her and his family.

His long journey is over. Shakespeare has shed London like a snakeskin. But several weeks hence he will be beckoned again by the siren song of the metropolis when the theatres re-open. Lured by the seductive drug of applause and laughter: approbation, esteem – and money.

But for a while, at least, London is far away.

The bust in Holy Trinity Church. 1911 Encyclopedia Britannica, vol. 24 plate 1, between pp 788 & 789. Photo: Harold Baker.

EPILOGUE

How did the England Shakespeare travel through differ from the one we have just traversed? We imagine the age of Elizabeth to be a golden era, one of freedom and expansion, the possibility of adventure filling the air. To a certain extent it was: after all, a glover's son could leave his father's trade and make a fortune from learning a craft that thousands would pay for. But the England Shakespeare's passed through was also an autocratic country, bound by law, custom and privilege. It was a country of low population – probably little more than two million. Even in a large town everyone would have known each other.

At first glance, little remains of the Elizabethan England Shakespeare would have passed through; but if one lingers a little as we have done, strolls more slowly rather than racing through the landscape in our saloon cars; focuses a more powerful lens on the streets, buildings and landscape one passes through, in short, practises an "archaeology of the eye," one can still find relics and echoes of the England of old that Shakespeare knew. As W.G. Hoskins said, "history is living all around us."

And the people? The folk he passed on his journey were so rooted in the earth and the rhythm of the seasons that they were almost pagan: the official religion may have been Church of England, but the rituals, superstitions, beliefs, were yet based on an ancient wisdom and custom handed down from the Saxons, the Romans, the Celts and beyond. The farmers, saddlers, ostlers, soldiers and innkeepers he spoke and ate with en route were more than acquaintances encountered on the road between ivory tower to home; they were his audience. And more than that, they were his characters.

For all his high poetry Shakespeare was the first great realist of English literature. And it was on the road from London to Stratford that he perhaps best saw the England whose character that became mirrored in his plays – the rough tavern speech, the swearing of a farmer, the drunken babbling of an ageing knight propping up a bar in some remote village; the bright intelligence of a Mistress Quickly running her brothel in a London rookery; the comical anecdotes of a man named Mouldy in the back-rooms of a tavern in Beaconsfield boasting of his soldierly prowess...

His journey home – like his touring, like his London tavern life, like his wit-combatting in the alehouses of Bishopsgate and Southwark - was part of the meat, drink and nourishment of his art – *("Ben Jonson and he did gather humours of men wherever they came,")* – and as we have accompanied him in this re-enactment, we may at least have glimpsed a faint shadow of the England that found its way into his writer's blood and brain.

www.ingramcontent.com/pod-product-compliance
Lightning Source LLC
Chambersburg PA
CBHW020418010526
44118CB00010B/313